The Mom's Guide to Asperger Syndrome*

*and related disorders

Jan Johnston-Tyler

APC

P.O. Box 23173
Shawnee Mission, Kansas 66283-0173
www.asperger.net

© 2007 Autism Asperger Publishing Co.
P.O. Box 23173
Shawnee Mission, Kansas 66283-0173
www.asperger.net

Publisher's Cataloging-in-Publication

Johnston-Tyler, Jan.
    The mom's guide to Asperger syndrome and related disorders / Jan Johnston-Tyler. -- 1st ed. -- Shawnee Mission, Kan. : Autism Asperger Pub. Co., 2007.

        p. ; cm.

        ISBN-13: 978-1-931282-42-0
        ISBN-10: 1-931282-42-0
        LCCN: 2007921491
        Includes bibliographical references and index.

        1. Asperger's syndrome in children. 2. Parents of autistic children. 3. Autism in children. I. Title.

RJ506.A9 J64 2007
618.92/858832--dc22   0703

Interior and cover design by Jan Johnston-Tyler.

This book is designed in Times Roman and Kristen.

Printed in the United States of America.

Table of Contents

Table of Contents

Chapter 5: The Oft-Dreaded IEP

Acknowledgments

Thank you!

I have been extraordinarily blessed to come across many professionals, advocates, and friends who have helped Will and me navigate this awesome world of Asperger Syndrome.

Among the people I would like to thank are the staff at Creative Children's Learning Center, who helped us realize Will had special needs; Dr. Lori Bond, who first diagnosed Will as having Asperger Syndrome; Bob Celeste, the principal at Will's school, who went above and beyond on many occasions to make sure Will was "successful throughout the school day;" Teresa Corfield, speech and language pathologist without peer; Rondalyn Whitney, whose occupational therapy and social skills classes were immensely helpful; Deborah Bloom, whose presence and thoughtful input helped me through a tough triennial review; and Dr. Maureen Hawkins, who took the time to understand my special son and help him through some very difficult times.

I'd also like to thank my good friend Mary Feliz for believing in me as an author, and for providing incredible feedback on

Chapter 1

the book, which I'm sure enhances its readability. And thanks to my colleague Stella Hackell for her excellent editing.

Finally, thanks to all my friends who stood by me and reached out to us, thanks to my family for supporting me in all I do, and thanks to my beautiful children, Will and Maia, who make my life rich and rewarding in every way.

–JJT

the book, which I'm sure enhances its readability. And thanks to my colleague Stella Hackell for her excellent editing.

Finally, thanks to all my friends who stood by me and reached out to us, thanks to my family for supporting me in all I do, and thanks to my beautiful children, Will and Maia, who make my life rich and rewarding in every way.

Chapter 1

Welcome to the World of Asperger Syndrome

Overview

This chapter explains what Asperger Syndrome is, what its effects are, how it is diagnosed, and some key history about the syndrome.

About This Book

This book is written primarily for parents and guardians of elementary school-age children who have been recently diagnosed with Asperger Syndrome (AS) or another closely related disorder, such as nonverbal learning disabilities (NLD) or high-functioning autism (HFA).

As the mom of an Asperger kid, I've lived through many trials and joys as I discovered what worked and what didn't work for us. Because there are only a handful of applicable, practical books on this disorder, and because this disorder seems to be on the rise (or at least its diagnosis is), I saw a need for real-life advice on how to parent a child with AS. Further, most books that are available are written either from a clinical perspective, or strictly from a personal perspective, such as *Elijah's Cup* by Valerie Paradiz (2002), *Eating an Artichoke* by Echo Fling (2000), *Finding Ben* by Barbara LaSalle (2004), and *My Andrew* by Wallis Simpson (2007).

While each book I've read on AS has helped me understand the syndrome better, what I wanted when we first got the diagnosis of AS was a single handbook with most of the information that I would need to help me formulate a comprehensive action plan while my son was in elementary school. I wanted a book that blended practical advice with personal insight, and that was written in a tone and format that I could easily refer to time and again. I have tried to write that book for all the parents of children with AS who come after me – I hope that this handbook becomes more and more dog-eared as you use it through the years.

But this book isn't just for parents. There is information here for nearly anyone who works with AS kids, or has the privilege to have one of these special children in their lives – teachers, friends, extended family members, and so on. While I take a definite "mom bias" here, and talk about my own experience from my own viewpoint, I'm confident that there is much information that you can use with the AS child in your world.

About Cheap Tricks

Throughout this book you will find Cheap Tricks sections meant to give you specific, easy solutions that really work.

What Is Asperger Syndrome?

You've picked up this book for a reason. I'll assume it's because you know someone who was recently diagnosed with AS, or someone you think has AS or who displays some of this disorder's features. Let's start by looking at the classic definition.

Diagnostic Definition

Asperger Syndrome is one of several disorders that fall on what is called the autism spectrum. Other related disorders include autism disorder, Rett's disorder, high-functioning autism, and nonverbal learning disorder (NLD), but not all of these disorders are classified as true diagnosable disorders in the United States at this time. What that means is that although clinicians, teachers, and psychologists recognize these as variants of autism, the *Diagnostic and Statistical Manual of Mental Disorders* (DSM-IV-TR) compiled by the American Psychiatric Association (APA, 2000), which is used for all official psychological diagnoses in the United States, does not call them out as specific disorders.

The Handbook of Autism and Pervasive Personality Disorders (Klin & Volkmar, 1997) describes the disorder like this:

> *Asperger Syndrome (AS) is a severe developmental disorder characterized primarily by marked and sustained difficulties in social interaction and emotional relatedness, and by unusual patterns of circumscribed interests and behavioral peculiarities.*

The DSM-IV-TR is used most frequently in the United States to diagnose mental disorders. The DSM-IV-TR classifies AS as belonging to the family of pervasive developmental disorders and describes its primary feature as "impairment in reciprocal social interaction," and notes that unlike autistic disorder, "there are no clinically significant delays in early language."

What all this means is that the primary noticeable symptom (called the presentation) of people with AS is that they have difficulty in social settings. They tend not to be able to read the social cues you and I take for granted, such as how close to stand to someone, how to engage in a back-and-forth conversation, when to look someone in the eye when speaking or listening, how to keep our bodies still when we are in a group setting, and so forth. Further, unlike neuro-typicals (people without the disorder), they usually cannot learn these skills naturally as part of maturation like other children do.

The diagnostic criteria for AS in the DSM-IV-TR (given the diagnostic code 299.80) are as follows:

A. Qualitative impairment in social interaction, as manifested by at least two of the following:

    1) Marked impairment in the use of multiple nonverbal behaviors such as eye-to-eye gaze, facial expression, body postures, and gestures to regulate social interaction

    2) Failure to develop peer relationships appropriate to developmental level

    3) A lack of spontaneous seeking to share enjoyment, interests, or achievements with other people (e.g., by a lack of showing, bringing, or pointing out objects of interest to other people)

    4) Lack of social or emotional reciprocity

B. Restricted repetitive and stereotyped patterns of encompassing preoccupation with one or more stereotyped and restricted patterns of interest that is either abnormal in intensity or focus

   1) Apparently inflexible adherence to specific, nonfunctional routines or rituals

   2) Stereotyped and repetitive motor mannerisms (e.g., hand or finger flapping or twisting, or complex whole-body movements)

   3) Persistent preoccupation with parts of objects

C. The disturbance causes clinically significant impairment in social, occupational, or other important areas of functioning.

D. There is no clinically significant general delay in language (e.g., single words used by age 2 years, communicative phrases by age 3 years).

E. There is no clinically significant delay in cognitive development or in the development of age-appropriate self-help skills, adaptive behavior (other than in social interaction), and curiosity about the environment in childhood.

F. Criteria are not met for another specific Pervasive Developmental Disorder or Schizophrenia.

These are the formal criteria that will most likely be used to diagnose your child with AS. Let's break this down a bit and look at examples of what the DSM-IV-TR criteria might look like in a child.

Qualitative Impairment in Social Interactions

This criterion describes the nonverbal language deficits kids with AS often have. For example, it is very common for AS kids to have little facial expression when speaking or being spoken to, either awkward or slumping body language (often leading teachers to think they are not paying attention), and a general inability to maintain eye contact when speaking or being spoken to. All of these characteristics make carrying on a conversation difficult for individuals with AS, as they are unable to read both facial expressions and body postures, and unable to exhibit appropriate expressions in return.

Further, many children with AS have a very difficult time developing friendships, and when they do, sometimes the friendship is one-sided, with the AS kid either being in control (such as with a younger child) or being subservient (such as with a child with a strong personality who bosses him around).

The criterion of "lack of spontaneous seeking to share enjoyment" can present itself in such ways as not being interested in rooting for the home baseball team with peers at a game, but insisting on talking about one's own personal hobbies. Children with AS also often have a hard time being good sports and cheering on another's victory, which can make participating in sports and P.E. very challenging for them.

The last characteristic described here is lack of reciprocity. In school-age children, this can manifest as failure to understand the social rules of play and friendship (such as inviting a kid they've never played with over for a sleepover that night at 7 p.m.) or an inability to understand why it's inappropriate to laugh at a peer's artwork in class.

A child must exhibit two of the above characteristics in order to meet the social impairment criterion.

Restricted Repetitive and Stereotyped Patterns of Behavior, Interests, and Activities

This criterion reflects the obsessive aspects of the disorder, whereby children often find a single theme, object, or idea, and become fixated on it. In school-age children, this one can be dicey to ferret out. Hundreds of thousands of little boys across the world are Pokémon aficionados, but only a fraction of them have AS. One way to tell if an intense interest qualifies as an obsession is to see how deeply fixated the child is. Does she talk to children, parents, teachers, or perfect strangers about her hobbies to the detriment of other social interaction? If so, it may be a sign.

Some kids with AS are also incredibly inflexible with regard to routine and need lots of warning when a well-set routine is going to be interrupted in order to prevent a meltdown. Other kids have more obsessive/compulsive mannerisms, such as insisting on lining up their shoes on the closet floor before leaving for school, always leaving a window opened a fraction of an inch before bedtime, and so forth.

Like more "classic" autistic children, kids with AS may exhibit some body motions that seem odd. Some kids rock back and forth. Others flap their hands or dance their feet while sitting down. These body motions are used most frequently when the kids are anxious or excited, and seem to help them "self-regulate" themselves by burning off excess physical energy so that they can focus mentally or calm themselves – an extreme form of fidgeting.

The persistent preoccupation with parts shows the difficulty these kids often have in understanding relatedness even with inanimate objects. In preschool, my son seemed to be fixated on the drainpipe under the sink as well as on the drain stopper, and repeatedly filled the sink and then let the water out as he tried to watch the water go down the drain. In the meantime, the other kids were busy having water fights, something that never occurred to him as being interesting.

Clinically Significant Impairment in Social, Occupational, or Other Important Areas of Functioning

This simply means that after meeting the first two criteria, there is evidence that these characteristics are impeding your child in some important way, such as making it difficult to make friends, to be successful in school, and so forth.

No Clinically Significant General Delay in Language (e.g., single words used by age 2 years, communicative phrases by age 3 years)

This means that classical autism has been ruled out, along with other language-delay-based disorders.

No Clinically Significant Delay in Cognitive Development or in the Development of Age-Appropriate Self-Help Skills, Adaptive Behavior (Other Than in Social Interaction), and Curiosity About the Environment in Childhood

This means that mental retardation has been ruled out (although in rare cases, there may be a dual diagnosis of AS along with mental retardation).

Criteria Are Not Met for Another Specific Pervasive Developmental Disorder or Schizophrenia

This means that these other disorders have been ruled out.

Other Diagnostic Tools

Although the DSM-IV-TR is widely used, it is not the only tool used to diagnose AS, and some practitioners would argue that it isn't even the best tool. Let's look at some other ways to detect AS.

In the *Handbook of Autism and Pervasive Personality Disorders* (1997), Klin and Volkmar list six sets of clinical criteria used to determine the presence of AS:

☐ Asperger (1944, 1979)

☐ Wing (1981)

☐ Gillberg and Gillberg (1989)

☐ Tantam (1988)

☐ Szatmari, Bremmer, and Nagy (1989)

☐ DSM-IV and DSM-IV-TR (1994, 2000)

Not all of these criteria sets are available to the lay person, but many can be found in public libraries or the libraries of universities with programs in psychology, if you find yourself interested in comparing the differences between them. The criteria sets of Asperger, Wing, Gillberg and Gillberg, and the DSM-IV-TR are all available, either free or for purchase, on the Internet. See *Resources* at the end of this book for more information.

There are other diagnostic tools that are probably more appropriate to the average parent. For those of us who are not credentialed PhD-level psychologists, Tony Attwood's *Asperger Diagnostic Assessment* DVD (2004) is a great resource (available at www.tonyattwood.com.au/).

A Lay Person's Guide to Common Symptoms

Asperger Syndrome has many different symptoms, and, to make matters more complicated, within this range of symptoms, there is a wide difference in the degree to which a given person is affected. Some children are profoundly affected, others very mildly so. This alone makes it difficult to accurately diagnose children. And because most of the diagnostic criteria are written for professionals, it can be bewildering to try to associate "restricted and stereotyped repetitive patterns" with what you're seeing in your son's kindergarten class.

To help you out, I have compiled an easy-to-understand listing of some of the more common and more broadly defined aspects of this disorder expressed in common language, as well as a simple checklist at the end of this section that contains common symptoms easily evaluated by non-PhDs.

Fixations

One of the most common symptoms is a tendency to have very strong attachments, sometimes mounting to obsessions (usually called a perseveration) on an item or a theme. Ask any mom of a kid with AS in grade school about Pokémon, and she'll probably roll her eyes and start thrashing on the ground. When she gets up and brushes herself off, she'll likely inform you that the only person who could have thought up Pokémon cards was someone who himself has AS! Now, not all kids who are Pokémon (or Yu Gi Oh or Naruto) freaks have AS. And not all elementary school-aged kids with AS love Pokémon (I have yet to find one who didn't, but I'm sure there's at least one out there).

So, even though your child can name all 500-plus Pokémon, tell you what each one's many evolutions and hit points are, and categorize them for you verbally via any number of taxonomies, this doesn't mean he has AS. But nearly every kid with AS has at least one phase in his life where he is absolutely fixated on a subject, learns everything he can about it, and then subjects anyone within a mile to his seemingly encyclopedic knowledge for hours on end. It may be dinosaurs, birds, motorcycles, or refrigerators. The obsessive love often changes as the child grows – and often just after you've finished redecorating his room in the now-dropped theme.

Lack of Perspective Taking

Another critical skill these kids don't have is perspective taking (i.e., being able to see the world from another person's perspective – to be in somebody else's shoes). This often manifests itself in an inability to read social cues and note when someone is no longer interested in a conversation. "If I'm this interested in a topic," reasons the AS child, "everyone else must be, too, because everyone thinks like I do."

A very sweet acquaintance of mine, who I suspect is an AS adult although he's never been diagnosed, presents by being unable to talk about anything but three subjects, over and over again. He seems unable to read visual cues suggesting that people are not listening to him, and even keeps talking once you have left the room. This tendency toward fixation coupled with an inability to know how to moderate a conversation can make individuals with AS very awkward conversationalists. Again, this alone does not mean a person is on the autism spectrum, but the behavior may warrant investigation.

Lack of Empathy

Lack of empathy is related to perspective taking, in that children with AS often have a hard time being sympathetic or empathic to somebody else's feelings. Recently, Will got in trouble at school for laughing at a classmate's artwork while the girl was giving an oral report. When I talked to him about it at home, he had difficulty understanding why this girl's feelings were hurt. "But the picture was funny, Mom. It just made me laugh. I didn't mean to hurt her feelings." If an AS kid thinks something is funny, he believes that everyone else finds it funny, too. He simply lacks the ability to see things from someone else's perspective.

Other instances include being bossy or domineering, difficulty in taking turns, or inappropriate name-calling. (I know that sounds odd, and while I do not condone any name-calling ever, there are age-related social standards by which it's okay to call someone an idiot, but it's not in the classroom in front of the teacher.) Kids with AS may also show aggression such as pushing and shoving. This characteristic can also manifest itself in an inability to purchase an appropriate gift and recognize the importance of social graces such as saying "please" and "thank you," writing thank-you cards, and the like.

Probably the biggest problem we've experienced in this area is helping Will understand when he needs to apologize, whether for accidentally stepping on someone's foot or inadvertently spilling paint on someone's artwork. It was easier teaching him to say "I'm sorry" when he did something wrong with intent, even though that took work, too. Far harder has been working with him to say he's sorry when he's done something accidentally. When I remind him that he needs to apologize, he asserts vehemently, "But it was an accident, Mom! I didn't mean to do it!" It's as if Will believes that the other child should automatically know that it was an accident, and that he is sorry, and that, therefore, it is redundant to say so. We are still working through the concept of responsibility for actions, regardless of motive. It's very hard for him to understand why he is responsible for another's feelings if he didn't intend to hurt them – lack of empathy in a nutshell.

All of these behaviors can add up to a child who looks rather antisocial and can cause great distress in social settings where the adults in charge (let alone the kids) don't understand what makes kids with AS tick. Your child may look like a little monster, and without intervention on your part, he may be ostracized.

Lack of Friends

Many kids with AS have few, if any, friends. Without intervention, these kids can be challenging to be around, and other children don't always have a lot of tolerance for what they perceive as aberrant behavior. In some cases, this can be devastating to the child with AS who craves social interaction and cannot figure out on her own why she isn't better liked. This can lead to depression and feelings of self-loathing.

Related to this, I've seen in my own son and in other similarly challenged kids a propensity for developing inappropriate friendships. This is frustrating for a parent to witness. Sometimes, more domineering kids attach themselves to a child with AS and more or less use him for their own fun.

A few years ago, a child with NLD whom I know was caught up in this sad game. Several kids thought it would be funny to make him spit on his shoe on command. They urged him repeatedly to do it, saying it would be fun. After a little prompting, the kid did it to the huge delight of the onlookers. Having made these kids laugh (and being unable to tell that they were laughing at him and not with him), he continued to spit, over and over again. On the one hand, this kid thought he had made a bunch of new friends with his trick and was beaming with delight that he had made them laugh. On the other hand, the kids were mocking him, treating him like a freak.

Children with AS also have a hard time navigating through a friendship once they make one, unable to understand the varying levels of friends, from acquaintance to friend to best friend. My son has repeatedly asked to invite a child for a sleepover when he has never even had a playdate with him, not understanding that first you have to play with somebody several times and then you can invite him for an overnight. The same problem has cropped up in developing invitation lists for birthday parties, where frequently the name of one or two kids with whom Will has never played pop up.

All of these rules of friendship are learned intuitively by most kids with little prompting from parents, but to a child with AS, they have to be taught and reinforced over and over again.

Lack of Verbal and Nonverbal Communication Skills

AS kids often suffer from severe communication issues beyond not being able to read social cues. Their tone of voice is often flat and without a lot of emotion, making them sound like robots. Coupled with little facial expression, this can make it hard to read their emotions. Other AS children speak too loudly; some have stilted speech in which unexpected words are emphasized. Not all kids demonstrate these characteristics, however.

Most children with AS are very literal. As a result, they often misunderstand phrases like "pull yourself up by the bootstraps" or "it's raining cats and dogs." This translates into difficulty with metaphors, jokes, double meanings, and the like, which can make schoolwork and recess very difficult for these children. Related to such literal-mindedness is inference, whereby a child has a hard time guessing the meaning of something by its relationship to something else. For example, in a book I read with him recently, Will could not guess the meaning of the word "rip-roaring" in the phrase "we had a rip-roaring good time at the party, eating our fill and dancing all night." Not only does this make social interactions difficult, it may play out in schoolwork as well, particularly in reading comprehension (they cannot infer subtle meanings or idioms used in a story) and in writing (their writing may be devoid of adjectives and adverbs).

Lack of Interest in Imaginative Play

Another hallmark of AS and related syndromes is a seeming inability to engage in imaginative play. This probably relates to the child's over-literalness, where a thing is just that thing, and nothing more. For example, a typical pre-schooler might spend hours building a Brio train setup, adding people, trees, buildings, and so on. He may spend even more hours playing, making the trains go, have passengers get on and off, making up stories about the passengers, and so on. A child with AS, by contrast, may get as far as building the train set (which may be very elaborate), but when it's built, it may cease to be interesting to him.

When Will was in preschool, he was obsessed with flannel-board stories, characters, and shapes cut out of felt that went with one of his favorite books or stories. He would beg me to make these for him to the point of almost driving me crazy. At the height of this frenzy, I had to set the limit of only making one a week. After about three months, I had made 16 sets of characters, from Eric Carle's *The Very Hungry Caterpillar*, to *Goldilocks and the Three Bears*. When each was done, Will would ask me to sit down with him and the flannel board, and have me retell the story to him, showing him all of the characters. And that was it. He would never play with them himself, nor was he terribly interested in hearing me tell the story again (though I would do so while working on the next masterpiece). He was merely interested in collecting them as objects.

Lack of Interest in Sports

Many kids with AS show a distinct lack of interest in organized sports. This is probably due to two factors: (a) the games require motor skills that these kids don't have in great quantity or quality; and (b) the fast play and complex rules overwhelm them. They can't process the information fast enough to keep up. Some kids manage to play an organized sport, such as soccer, but I've only known one AS child becoming a real jock. This can be very difficult in our culture, where there is a strong emphasis on kids playing organized sports, and competition in general, and can lead to an AS kid feeling like he does not fit in.

Sports that these kids tend to be good at (that don't overwhelm them, even if they never end up excelling at them) are individual sports such as swimming, martial arts, and tennis.

Lack of Organizational Skills

Many kids with AS have problems keeping their stuff together, whether it is losing GameBoy cartridges at home or organizing their paperwork at school. They lack the ability to set up and maintain an orderly system in the physical world, and even if they do, they have difficulty adhering to the system under the normal duress of school, moving classrooms, changing periods, and so forth.

This is equally frustrating for all involved – teachers, parents, and the child. The teachers are working with many other students and can't always stop to help the child with AS find his missing assignment. The child, rushing to his next class or study session, gets frustrated by not being able to find anything in his almost-certainly messy desk or backpack. Parents aren't there to help and support but can only help with homework that actually makes it home. What happens to this paperwork between the time the teacher hands it out and the child gets home is a mystery to most parents.

Kids with AS also have a hard time managing their time (e.g., planning ahead to make sure that an assignment is done on time and properly) and organizing their work. And organizational difficulties show up in the schoolwork itself. For example, many have difficulty writing a theme paper that includes all the necessary parts (beginning, middle, end) along with reasonable transitions between "bits" of information. This shows the difficulties these kids have with both weakness in language and weakness in organization.

Bare-Bones Asperger Syndrome Checklist

While the following checklist in no way replaces formal diagnosis by a trained professional, it may help you to identify whether or not you need to engage a professional for assessment and possible diagnosis. Note that most AS kids do not have all of these symptoms, or have them only very mildly.

Functional Area	Manifestation	Your Ratings & Comments
Social	Lacks friends or doesn't make friends easily.	
	Repetitive in play; does the same thing over and over again.	
	Avoids eye contact.	
	Talks like an "encyclopedia" about one or more topics.	
	Doesn't understand rules of personal space or boundaries.	
	Is rude without intention; doesn't understand social rules.	
	Either takes offense mistakenly, or is unaware of another's attempt to hurt or embarrass.	
	Cannot have a back-and-forth conversation. Talks on about a topic or a set of facts that is not of interest to the listener.	
	Does not ask questions of "interest" such as where a person lives, or what he likes to do.	
	Lacks facial expression and speech intonation. Speaks in a monotone.	
	Has meltdowns over seemingly insignificant events.	
	Especially when young, may feel it is appropriate to cheat in games. Has difficulty following or learning the rules of play.	

Functional Area	Manifestation	Your Ratings & Comments
Cognitive (Learning)	Has near-photographic memory.	
	Is very literal. Has difficulty inferring meaning, often making literature comprehension and humor difficult.	
	Has difficulty with abstract thought and generalizing learned information from one situation to another.	
	Excels in math and science.	
	Appears not to be paying attention in class due to lack of eye gaze and slumped posture.	
	Has difficulty in managing time (e.g., in test taking) and keeping schoolwork/desk organized.	
	Does not ask for help when needed. Gets stuck easily.	
Behaviors	Has unusual or extreme fears.	
	Excessively "hates" the way some things feel, taste, look, sound, or smell.	
	Has trouble either sitting still (fidgets, rocks, taps foot) or maintaining an "awake" (upright) position.	
	Has difficulty with fine-motor skills, such as learning to write neatly, tying shoes, artwork.	
	Has difficulty with gross-motor skills, such as learning to ride a bike, running, jumping, playing ball.	

Other Bits and Bites

AS is primarily a boy's diagnosis. It is found in more males than females at a rate of 5 to 1 (Ehler and Gillberg's research in 1993 showed it was as high as 10 to 1). AS seems to have a hereditary component, and often one parent will exhibit some Asperger-like characteristics, such as social shyness or being intensely analytical. The disorder cannot be cured; it is a lifetime disorder. While this sounds dire, early and proper intervention can make a profound difference. Unlike many people with classical autism, kids with AS nearly always grow up to be able to lead fulfilling and productive lives.

Confusion in the Clinical World

Part of the reason for the various diagnostic tools mentioned earlier in the chapter is that AS can be difficult to diagnose. As mentioned, there are a variety of symptoms, each of which also ranges in severity. Further, there is confusion in the professional world between nonverbal language disorder (NLD), attention deficit/hyperactive disorder (ADHD), and what is sometimes called high-functioning autism (HFA). Also, a child may present with different aspects at different stages in his life.

Your child may or may not exhibit all of the characteristics using any diagnostic tool. Or your child may exhibit one or more of these characteristics, but may not receive a diagnosis of AS. Regardless of what diagnosis you receive, if your child presents with any of these symptoms, he or she should be receiving some sort of intervention. As a parent, your job is to teach your child to become a self-sufficient adult. If you have a child with AS, your role is slightly more difficult than that of other parents, but that much more important.

Diagnosis for Securing Services

Because of the clinical confusion, a child may receive a diagnosis from one professional of ADHD, later receive a diagnosis of NLD, and yet later be diagnosed as having AS. Ironically, all of these diagnoses may be accurate, in whole or in part, at the time of diagnosis. Diagnosing your child may feel like capturing a rain cloud in a bottle. You know it's in there, but it evaporates before your eyes and changes into something else. The diagnostic process can be exceedingly frustrating for parents who are trying to secure services for their child. While I'm not big on labels per se, without a diagnosis, it can be very, very difficult to convince educators to provide services for your child.

I don't believe it is wrong to tell a professional diagnostician that you are trying to get help for your child and that your school district will not budge in giving services until you have a formal diagnosis. Most professionals are well aware of how hard it can be to secure services, and if they think there is some help to be gleaned from intervention, they will want to ensure that your child receives the help he needs. (See Assessments later in this book for more information on this topic.)

A Brief History of the Disorder

Asperger Syndrome was named for Hans Asperger, a Viennese pediatrician (*see* http://en.wikipedia.org/wiki/Hans_Asperger), who in the 1940s worked with boys who had autism. He noted that some of these children had abnormal fixations and experienced difficulty fitting in socially with their peers. He also noted that these children often had special capacities for independent thinking and high intelligence, prompting him to refer to them as "little professors." At the same time in Boston, an American psychologist named Leo Kanner (*see* http://en.wikipedia.org/wiki/Leo_Kanner) was working with a group of children who were described as autistic, but had slight differences from the classic definitions of autism. In 1943, he described the features of what he called "early childhood autism" as the following:

- ❐ profound autistic withdrawal

- ❐ an obsessive desire for the preservation of sameness

- ❐ a good rote memory

- ❐ an intelligent and pensive expression

- ❐ mutism or language without real communicative intent

- ❐ over-sensitivity to stimuli

- ❐ a skillful relationship with objects

Both of these gentlemen's works fell into obscurity after World War II, until a researcher named Lorna Wing compared these works in the 1980s and found striking similarities, both in what they described in the children they worked with and in how they had differentiated this disorder from classical autism.

Wing's criteria for what she named Asperger Syndrome included the following:

- ❐ impairment of two-way social interaction and general social ineptitude

☐ speech that is odd and pedantic, stereotyped in content, but is not delayed

☐ limited nonverbal communication skills – little facial expression or gesture

☐ resistance to change and enjoyment of repetitive activities

☐ circumscribed special interests and good rote memory

☐ poor motor coordination, with odd gait and posture and some motor stereotypes.

Later, in 1990, a group of researchers, Baron-Cohen, Leslie, and Frith, went on to describe a characteristic of autism that they called "mind-blindness." This characteristic was demonstrated by an experiment known as "The Sally-Ann test" (Wimmer & Perner, 1983, in Happé, 1994, p. 40) , which demonstrated that children with autism lacked the ability to predict others' behavior or perspective. In this test, each child was shown two dolls. Sally has a basket and Anne has a box. In the story, enacted in front of the tested child, Sally "puts" a marble in her basket while Anne is "watching." Then Sally "goes for a walk." While she is out, Anne "puts" the marble in Anne's box. Then Sally "returns."

The child is then asked, "Where will Sally look for her marble?" The correct answer, of course, is "in her basket," because that's where Sally should "believe" her marble still is, not having "seen" Anne move it to her box. However, children with autism answer "in the box" because they are not capable of "seeing reality" through Sally's eyes.

In 1994, the American Psychiatric Association adopted the term Asperger Disorder and refined the diagnostic criteria, published in the *Diagnostic and Statistical Manual of Mental Disorders*.

Because AS is a relatively new diagnosis, the professional world is in catch-up mode to refine the definition and treatment of this disorder. This in itself may be the reason, in whole or in part, why diagnosis of this disorder is rising dramatically. There have probably always been kids with AS. Remember the student in your class with the broken glasses who ran the projector in AV Club, only had one or two friends, and could never climb to the top of the rope in gym? Could he have had AS? Maybe. Now instead of calling them "spazzes," "geeks," or "nerds," we can try to understand and respect them for who they truly are.

What Causes Asperger Syndrome?

As confusing as the look of Asperger Syndrome is, the likely causes of this disorder are just as maddeningly unclear.

Theories abound. I've read articles purporting that autism is caused by neurochemical imbalances in the brain or by brainstem abnormalities as evidenced in autopsies of people with autism. And I've read equally weighty and well-researched articles that disprove both of these theories.

One prevalent theory is that AS in particular (and autism in general) is related to childhood immunizations, which has caused many parents in the United States not to immunize their children. Even Robert Kennedy, Jr., has put forth the theory that the U.S. government knows that autism is caused by Thimerosal, a preservative used in vaccinations until recently ("Deadly Immunity," retrieved December 30, 2006, from http://dir.salon.com/story/news/feature/2005/06/16/thimerosal/index_np.html). The American Medical Association thoroughly rejects this notion.

Another theory is that children with AS may have been deprived of oxygen during birth or that autism may be caused by food allergies (information retrieved November 14, 2006, from http://home.iprimus.com.au/rboon/Aspergers.htm).

What most researchers seem to agree on is that the disorder may be passed from generation to generation, and that parents with one child with a disorder on the autism spectrum have a higher chance of having another child with a similar disorder. Further, one or both parents, while not having autism themselves, may have one or more characteristics of the disorder, be they social shyness or deep analytical tendencies.

Overall, most mainstream sources of medical research believe that while there is almost certainly a genetic component, more research needs to be conducted to determine if there are any environmental or other contributing factors (see MRC Review of Autism Research: Epidemiology and Causes [2001], retrieved December 30, 2006, from http://www.mrc.ac.uk/Utilities/Documentrecord/index.htm?d=MRC002394).

Clearly, we have a lot more to learn about this disorder.

References

American Psychiatric Association. (2000). *Diagnostic and Statistical Manual of Mental Disorders IV-T*R (4th ed.). Washington, DC: Author.

Asperger, H. (1944). Die "Autistischen Psychopathen" im Kindesalter. *Archiv fur Psychiatrie und Nervenkrankheiten, 117*, 76-136.

Asperger, H. *Hans Asperger*. Retrieved December 30, 2006, from http://en.wikipedia.org/wiki/Hans_Asperger.

Attwood, T. *Asperger's Diagnostic Assessment*. Retrieved December 30, 2006, from http://www.tonyattwood.com.au/.

Boon, R. *Asperger's Syndrome: Causes*. Retrieved October 16, 2006, from http://home.iprimus.com.au/rboon/Aspergers.htm

Cumine, V., Leach, J., & Stevenson, G. (1998). *Asperger Syndrome: A practical guide for teachers*. London: David Fulton Publishers.

Ehlers, S., & Gillberg, C. (1993, Nov). The epidemiology of Asperger Syndrome – A total population study. *Journal of Child Psychology and Psychiatry and Allied Disciplines, 34*(8), 1327-1350.

Fling, E. (2000). *Eating an artichoke: A mother's perspective on Asperger Syndrome*. London: Jessica Kingsley Publishers.

Frith, U. (2001, Dec.). Mind blindness in the brain in autism. *Neuron, 32*(6), 969-979.

Frith, U. (Ed.). (1991). *Autism and Asperger Syndrome*. Cambridge, UK: Cambridge University Press.

Gillberg, I. C., & Gillberg, C. (1989). Asperger syndrome– some epidemiological considerations: A research note. *Journal of Child Psychology and Psychiatry, 30*, 631-8.

Happé, F. (1994). *Autism: An introduction to psychological theory*. London: UCL Press.

Kanner, L., & Eisenberg, L. (1956). Early infantile autism 1943-1955. *American Journal of Orthopsychiatry, 26*, 55-65.

Kanner, L. *Leo Kanner*. Retrieved December 30, 2006, from http://en.wikipedia.org/wiki/Leo_Kanner

Kennedy, R., Jr. (2005). *Deadly immunity*. Retrieved October 16, 2006, from http://dir.salon.com/story/news/feature/2005/06/16/thimerosal/print.html

Klin, A., & Volkmar, F. (1997). *Handbook of autism and pervasive developmental disorders* (2nd ed.). New York: John Wiley & Sons, Inc.

LaSalle, B. (2004). *Finding Ben: A mother's journey through the maze of Asperger's.* New York: MacGraw Hill.

MRC Review of Autism Research: Epidemiology and Causes. (2001). What are the causes of autism spectrum disorders? (pp. 21-47). London: Medical Research Council.

Paradiz, V. (2002). *Elijah's cup: A family's journey into the community and culture of high-functioning autism and Asperger's Syndrome.* New York: Free Press.

Szatmari, P., Bremmer, R., & Nagy, J. N. (1989a). Asperger's Syndrome: A review of clinical features. *Canadian Journal of Psychiatry, 34*(6), 554-560.

Simpson, W. (2007). *My Andrew: Day-to-day living with a child with an autism spectrum disorder.* Shawnee Mission, KS: Autism Asperger Publishing Company.

Tantam, D. (1988). Annotation: Asperger's syndrome. *Journal of Child Psychology and Psychiatry, 29*, 836-40.

Wing, L. (1981). Asperger's syndrome: A clinical account. *Psychological Medicine, 11*, 115-130.

Chapter 2

The Diagnosis

The mere word *diagnosis* is scary. We tend to associate it with life-threatening illnesses such as cancer and may find ourselves wondering if we really want to know what is wrong. Maybe it's easier to live with the possibility of something being wrong than the certitude of facts. Maybe we're just imagining things.

This chapter talks about when to turn for help from a diagnostician and what the process is like. If you suspect something is wrong, it's time to get answers.

When You Suspect Something Is Wrong

There is probably nothing more frightening than thinking there is something wrong with your child. You may have noticed that your child doesn't have many friends or that she acts differently from the other kids at school. You may have noticed that your child melts down every day after coming home from school or that he finds ways to be late to school each day. The stuffed animals and "lovies" that were cute when he was three might have turned into near-obsessions at age seven.

All of these signals can create extreme distress for you and those around you. What do you do when you think something might be wrong?

A Diagnostic Journey

I'll never forget the day the director of my son's preschool called and told me that she wanted me to come in to talk about my son. We had already been kicked out of one day-care program because of Will's biting and tantrums. I was fearful that the same thing was about to happen again. He had made no friends and never played with other children. Although very verbal, when he was stressed, he couldn't find his words and would bite other children when they got too close or tried to take a toy away from him.

Transitions (drop-off and pick-up) were torturous, often ending in tears – both his and mine. Changes in routine would send him over the edge, and teachers often reported that they had to pick him up and physically move him from room to room because he could not be coerced to move on his own. In contrast, Will was often described by teachers as a wonderfully sweet, attentive, intelligent child, with a great laugh and a love for hugs. As a parent, I was at my wits' end. Who was this child? He was so confusing!

When I met with the director, I was relieved when she immediately told me that despite repeated biting incidents (one parent asked if my child had had his shots, as if he were a dog), the staff felt that this was not a disciplinary issue but something different.

The teachers noted Will's lack of shift from parallel play (common up until age 3) to reciprocal (interactive) play. They noted his awkward attempts to engage other children in play, such as knocking over a child's castle built out of blocks. Most chilling, perhaps, his teacher described how one day Will would not leave the class for the playground until he had lined up the dinosaurs on the windowsill just so, each dinosaur equidistant from those on either side and all facing in the same direction at the exact same angle. Once this task was done, he happily skipped out of the room. He was 4 at the time.

The daycare staff recommended that I call the Children's Health Council in Palo Alto, California, where we lived, and ask for an intake consultation. After a few visits with one PhD in psychology, we were referred to another, who specialized in AS. After many tests and observations, Will received a preliminary diagnosis of AS. Our journey had begun.

This is what Asperger Syndrome looked like to us when Will was 4. Your diagnostic journey may look different. You may note inflexibility in routine, obsession with an item, hobby, or theme, encyclopedic knowledge on a given subject, or inability to interact with peers in an age-appropriate way. Like us, you may also note anxiety in large groups, discomfort around loud noises, and a lack of creative or imaginative play (which, ironically, Will acquired in full force at around age 8). AS looks different in different kids, at different ages, and in different situations.

If, as in my case, your AS child is your first child, it may be difficult to assess just how different your child is. Rely on the criteria and specialists, along with confidential talks with people (your family, friends, and teachers) who know your child well, and preferably have children of their own.

When you suspect AS or another autism spectrum disorder, read the diagnostic criteria in the section "What Is Asperger Syndrome?" to see if there are enough matches to warrant a visit to a specialist.

How to Find the Resources You Need

Before you start looking for a professional to help assess and possibly diagnose your child, it's worth understanding who the potential professionals are, how they are credentialed, and how they can help you and your child and at what stage of the process.

The Diagnosis Is Only the Beginning!

Securing a diagnosis is not enough. Afterward you'll need to find experts who can help you sort out your child's behavior so that you can take appropriate steps to help him. Finding good resources is key.

The Differences Between Psychiatrists, Clinical Psychologists, Psychologists, Counselors, and Social Workers

There are many types of professionals who can help you and your child before and after a diagnosis of Asperger Syndrome. The titles and credential requirements vary from state to state, but the following chart provides a general idea of the various "degrees of degrees" and services available.

Title	Education/Licensing Requirements	Services Provided
Psychiatrist	MD plus a specialization in psychiatry	Testing and assessment Diagnoses Pharmacological treatment Therapeutic interventions*
Clinical Psychologist, PhD	Doctorate degree in psychology; in most states, needs to hold a state license to practice	Testing and assessment Diagnoses Therapeutic interventions
Clinical Psychologist, MA or MS	Master's degree in psychology, additional requirements vary by state; in most states, needs to hold a state license to practice	Testing and assessment Diagnoses Therapeutic interventions
Counseling Psychologist, Therapist, MA or MSW	Master's degree in counseling psychology or social work, additional requirements vary by state; in most states, must hold a specialized state license to practice	Testing and assessment Diagnoses* Therapeutic interventions
Social Worker, Therapist, BA	Bachelor's degree in social work or psychology, additional requirements vary by state. Must hold a specialized state license to practice.	Diagnoses* Therapeutic interventions

* *These services may not be provided by a given professional. Check to see what a person's expertise is before expecting these services.*

Only a psychiatrist can prescribe drugs for your child, and only psychiatrists, and psychologists at a master's level or greater, can perform testing and assessment to formally diagnosis AS following the criteria in the DSM-IV-TR. Therefore, if you are seeking a formal diagnosis or are looking into medication for your child, you will need to work with an appropriately credentialed professional.

Any of these professionals might be helpful to your child depending on your situation and your child's needs. For example, a social worker with a specialty and years of experience in autism spectrum disorders will likely provide far greater help to your family than a psychiatrist with little or no expertise in this area.

Hiring a Professional to Diagnose Your Child

Now that you have an idea of what the disorder looks like, and have gotten a taste of the types of professionals who can help you secure a diagnosis, let's look at why it is so important to take this first step now, rather than later.

Why a Diagnosis Is Crucial

A rose by any other name is still a rose, and your young flower will bloom based on interventions, not based on a diagnosis. So, why is it important to get a formal diagnosis from a credentialed and credible professional? Because, as mentioned earlier, you may be required to have verifiable proof of your child's diagnosis to secure services from your school district. And while the school district will likely ask for a second opinion (at their cost), your money will not be wasted.

School districts have limited funds and many children who need special interventions, so they cannot afford to help every child with what they see as a minor problem. Therefore, any issues your child may have must be deemed to be clinically significant in order to merit intervention in the school setting. This means that it is in the best interest of the district to give services only to those who truly need them. Thus, it may behoove them to try to disprove your independent diagnosis or to prove that, regardless of a diagnosis, your child's issues are not clinically significant (e.g., do not make him "unsuccessful throughout the school day").

It may sound cold-hearted, but our schools are woefully underfunded, and the officials responsible for offering special education to children must watch every penny lest a truly deserving child go without (lest they drive the entire district into debt in order to maintain services). More information on what your child is legally entitled to is found in Chapter 4.

In short, get a solid diagnosis by a credible professional. It's worth your energy and your money.

Interviewing Professionals

There are a number of ways to find people who work with kids on the autism spectrum, from the Internet to parent groups to your pediatrician to the local school district. You can start by looking in the Resources & References section to get ideas on where to begin.

Compile a list of three to five professionals, and ask each of them to speak to you over the phone so you can ask them some questions. Here is a brief list to start; modify it for your own use.

- ❐ Do you specialize in children on the autistic spectrum?

- ❐ How long have you worked with children on the spectrum?

❏ Given a diagnosis of Asperger Syndrome, what interventions do you typically recommend?

❏ How successful have these interventions been?

❏ Have you ever worked with my child's school district?

❏ Have you ever worked with any local AS groups and, if so, which one(s)?

Possibly more important than the answers is the rapport you feel with this person. Does this feel like someone you can trust? Is she compassionate and willing to give of her time, or is she rushed and self-inflated? There are times when you want the very best person on the block, no matter how awkward his bedside manner. However, when it is feasible, choose someone you can work with, as this person will be a great ally to you and your child in the future.

The Assessment

Once you've found a person who can help you with your child's assessment and diagnosis, call and ask for an intake session to begin the process. Several methods and tools are used to assess for autism spectrum disorders, but most assessments will contain these elements:

❏ An interview with one or both parents

❏ Parent assessment forms

❏ Teacher/caretaker assessment forms

❏ Informal observation of the child in play (in the waiting room or in school, for example)

❏ Formal observation of the child through direct play and conversation

❏ Formal assessment through written or oral tests

In larger settings, such as a hospital or children's center, you may be allowed to watch your child through a one-way mirror while he is being interviewed and tested. If your child is overly anxious, the diagnostician will likely allow you to stay in the room, provided it is not disruptive to the process. Depending on the types of tests being administered (refer to "Overview of Commonly Used Tests" later in this book), the process can run up to two or three sessions, an hour or more per session.

After the diagnostician has collected information through assessment and observation, she will write up her findings in a full psychological and behavioral report, which should include test scores, observed behavioral issues, and information about the child's current level of disability. Often, she will ask the parents to come back into the office to discuss this report with them directly.

A Word About Priming

Before your child undergoes any assessment or testing, you will need to talk to him about what the process is about. Children with Asperger Syndrome tend to be very sensitive to changes in their daily routine. I suggest that you sit with your child the day before any assessment and explain to him, in age-appropriate language, what will happen, how long it will take, and what you hope to learn from the assessment. This "priming" will help him cope with a new, and possibly uncomfortable, experience.

Formal and Preliminary Diagnoses

Generally speaking, there are two types of diagnoses:

❑ A preliminary diagnosis may be given to a very young child (under 7, generally) who shows strong tendencies toward AS. This diagnosis is useful because full-blown AS usually is not recognized as being diagnosable until 7 or 8 years of age. If your diagnostician is uncomfortable diagnosing your young child, ask him or her for a preliminary diagnosis, with a follow-up, formal diagnosis when your child is around 8 years of age. Most professionals will comply. Additionally, some professionals will give a more general diagnosis to young children, such as pervasive personality disorder-not otherwise specified (PPD-NOS), stating that their belief is that the child will later test as having AS.

❑ A formal diagnosis simply means that a child has been tested, assessed, and observed, and that all of the information gleaned by the professional has led him or her to a diagnosis of Asperger Syndrome (or a related disorder) as described in the DSM-IV.

Receiving the Diagnosis and Asking Questions

When you meet with the diagnostician after assessment, one of three things will happen: (a) the diagnostician will give you a written report with his or her findings showing no clinically significant problems (hence, no diagnosis); (b) the diagnostician will give you a diagnosis along with the report; or (c) the diagnostician will give you the report with no diagnosis and recommend that your child be seen by another specialist for further testing. This latter usually happens if the diagnostician is a generalist and wants your child to be seen by a specialist to test in other specific areas.

Before the meeting, prepare a list of questions. You'll want to learn how to get your child adequate services – what kind and from whom – if you receive a diagnosis of AS or a related syndrome.

No Diagnosis – When to Get a Second Opinion

You did everything right. You called three professionals, you picked one with fabulous credentials and a great personality, but the person decided that there's nothing wrong with your child. Or thinks that something entirely different is wrong with your child. Or (and yes, this happens) thinks there is something wrong with you.

Take a long walk. Talk to your friends. Talk to your spouse. Talk to the cat. Maybe you really are seeing spots where none exists. If so, that's okay. Be relieved that your child is fine. If, however, after some good, old-fashioned self-reflection, you are certain, or even pretty darn sure, that this professional is wrong, get a second opinion.

You have to trust your gut on this. Professionals slip up. They have bad days. And, your child (if typically Asperger-like) has particularly good days, and maybe the professional saw that child, not the one who sits under the picnic table at school and cries because everyone calls him a geek.

Another time you might want to get a second opinion is if the school district has gotten a diagnosis for your child with which you disagree. As mentioned before, kids with AS often get diagnosed as ADHD before the AS is discovered. While some of the interventions for ADHD might help an AS child, they will likely not go far enough for your child, and you'll need some ammunition to prove it.

Treatment Plan

Regardless of what type of diagnostician you see, once a diagnosis has been made, the diagnostician should work with you to develop a written treatment plan that is age-appropriate and suitable for your child's specific needs. Because you know your child better than anyone, you should have some input into what services he should receive.

For example, if your child is sweet and doesn't disobey or get into trouble, you don't need to work on defiant behavior (although many AS parents will need help here). If your child has a very difficult time in transitions between home and school, this is an area for improvement and should be part of the plan. Think about what life is like for your child, where the problem areas are, and make sure that they are accounted for in your child's treatment plan.

Two Words of Advice

First, pick your battles. If your child has many issues that need work, pick a few of the most severe ones to work on now, and let the others slide for a bit. Your child will resist being completely made over (wouldn't you?) and you'll wear yourself out trying.

An alternate tactic is to pick the low-hanging fruit – work on something you think your child can do quickly and easily, which will demonstrate to him that he can be successful in changing his behavior. This will give you something to use to encourage future efforts: "Remember how well you did at remembering to say 'please and thank you' at Gramma's house? You can learn this, too."

Second, remember that your child is just a kid! All parents work on teaching their kids to be self-sufficient adults. Just because your child has AS doesn't mean that every aspect of his personality needs to be part of a treatment plan. If he acts bratty and bossy to his little sister, this may just be part of being a kid, and not due to the disorder. It could be just a plain parenting job and may not need to be part of the treatment plan. Use your common sense.

Following are some typical aspects of a treatment plan for a child with AS.

Area of Weakness	Intervention	Potential Provider
Weak eye gaze	Speech pragmatics therapy (helps your child communicate socially)	Speech-language pathologist (SLP; may also be a special education teacher, but should be someone who has studied speech pragmatics)
Lack of reciprocity in conversation	Speech pragmatics therapy	SLP
Perseveration on a given topic	Speech pragmatics therapy, social skills groups, redirection at home	SLP, children's services organization, parents
Transitioning	Classroom intervention, redirection by parents	Teachers, SLP, parents
Lack of interactive play and/or friends	Social skills group	SLP, children's services organization, parents
Disruptive in class	Speech pragmatics therapy or behavioral therapy	SLP, general education teacher, behavioral therapist

Recommendations

After receiving a diagnosis of Asperger Syndrome and reviewing a potential treatment plan with the diagnostician, your next question is likely to be, "Okay, now what?"

Depending on where you live, services for your child may be easy or difficult to secure. Your diagnostician should be able to provide you with a list of places to look for services, as well as give you some basic information on how to request an individualized education program (IEP) if one is warranted.[1]

Getting recommendations from your professional is one of the best ways to start, as he or she probably knows some of the best people in the area who can help you. If you can't get a list of providers, advice on how to secure these services is found in the Resources & References section of this book.

Follow-Up Services

As mentioned earlier, you may be referred to another specialist for further testing and evaluation or for specific services. For example, children with AS who are suffering from severe depression or major behavioral issues in or out of the classroom may be referred to a psychiatrist for further testing or to be screened as a candidate for mood-altering drugs. Your child may also be referred to another specialist such as a speech therapist or behaviorist as part of his treatment plan.

---

1. An IEP is a tailored educational program for children with special needs. These programs are governed by federal law, and as such can be quite complicated. Refer to the chapter The Oft-Dreaded IEP for more information.

To Tell or Not to Tell

As you are going through the diagnostic process, and certainly once you have secured a diagnosis, you need to decide what you will tell your child. This is something to spend some time thinking about. You may also want to talk about it with someone you trust and respect before making your decision on how to handle this delicate situation.

What Your Child Needs to Know

Even very young children will show interest or curiosity when you take them to see a clinician for testing. While some parts of the diagnosis are likely to rely on discreet observation of the child, more of it will rely on intelligence, speech, and behavior testing. Any child will want to know why you are taking her to see a doctor who asks lots of questions. Before going in, be prepared with a plan of what you will tell your child. You may want to role play with your spouse or a good friend ahead of time to make sure you're covering all bases.

A Bias Toward Truth-Telling

I have to admit that I have a very strong bias toward truth-telling, when appropriate. One of the hallmarks of AS is high intelligence. These kids tend to be very smart and inquisitive. If left to their own devices, they can come up with some pretty outlandish, and often self-destructive, ideas about their limitations (of which they are often painfully aware) that can further degrade their self-esteem.

Although we didn't tell Will the label for the disorder, I decided to tell him at age 4 what we had learned from his assessment. I told him that we had learned that it was a little harder for him to make friends and a little harder to sit still in class, but emphasized that his differences were minor, and that in most ways, he was just like everyone else. The teaching moment then, and now, is that everyone is different in some way, and that's the way life is. Our differences make us unique and special.

The Right to Know – You Have Asperger Syndrome

When Will was 8 years old and was being retested as part of his first triennial IEP review, I decided the time was right to tell him he had Asperger Syndrome. Several people have flapped their arms over my telling my son he had AS, even though I assured them that I had done so using age-appropriate language in a positive, reaffirming, reassuring way.

"You're labeling your child!" they exclaimed. "He'll be marked for life!"

I thought, "Oh, really?" Would it be better that he thought that he was to blame for his inability to make friends and sit still?

That's often what happens when a child is different and the adults in his life fail to tell him why. And it was exactly what happened to my son. He knew he was different. He knew that the other kids perceived him as being different. Without a logical explanation, he was left with only one alternative to explain his struggles: "I'm no good."

It crushed me to hear him say this, over and over. And no amount of reassuring him that he was just different worked. He had reached the age of needing more information about how he was different and why, so it seemed appropriate to tell him.

One of the earmarks of good mental health is the ability to know your limitations, and to accept them in a self-loving way as part of who you are – striving to overcome them, perhaps, but to accept yourself as is.

I am mathematically challenged. I have taken remedial courses, read math books on my own, but still cannot grasp anything past algebra. It's just part of who I am, and as long as I can balance my checkbook, multiply a recipe by three, write up a financial report, and understand the stock market and my 401(k) plan, I'm okay. I know my limitations. The world of calculus seems to be okay without my active participation.

So, why are children different? It is important to ensure that your child knows that a limitation in one area usually means that she has a significant benefit in another. Your child needs to know that she is loved unconditionally by you and by the other important people in her life. Your child needs to be reassured that there is a place for her in this world and that she is worthy and plays a meaningful role. Your child needs to be told that this information should only be shared with family and close friends. But most important, your child needs to know that there is nothing wrong with her.

This is a very important point. In our society, there is a pervasive attitude that different equates to bad or wrong. I would argue that this is a socially imposed, and quite artificial and harmful, attitude that causes a world of social woes, from racial inequality to gender bias to class elitism.

I would further argue that if your child had a broken leg, were blind, had dyslexia, or suffered from diabetes, no one would criticize you for explaining to your child, in age-appropriate terms, what his limitations were and how you as the parent were going to help him overcome this small limitation in the bigger world. Why would you not tell the child about AS? Simply put, many people advise you not to tell children because there is social stigma associated with it.

Chapter 2

A year ago, a friend of mine received a report from a well-known psychologist who specializes in AS. She had been through several specialists and had yet to receive a solid diagnosis of her son's difficulties. She was very distressed with the report. She read it to me over the phone. One part of it still raises my hackles. In this passage, the psychologist retold how during an interview about friends, this child told the doctor that he had a good friend who had AS, and how they got along really well because they liked the same things like Pokémon. They were so much alike and they didn't mind each other's "silly stuff." He told the doctor that he was very happy to have another kid he could talk to confidentially about his differences and difficulties, who understood what it was like to be different in some ways. They were, he added, best friends.

Now stop for a moment. As a parent of a child with AS, what would your reaction be? Likely, "Wow, how lucky these two kids found each other, and have built an alliance in their similarities! This is great!"

Guess what the doctor said? That she was "horrified" (yes, horrified!) that this child (my son, at the time age 9) had been told that he had AS and was therefore labeled for life. She went on to chide my parenting skills in another child's report! How audacious is that? Would this same doctor chide a parent for telling her daughter that she had diabetes? Would she think it was inappropriate if this child had found a good friend who also had diabetes, and they were able to talk about what it was like having certain differences?

Emphatically, no.

No professional of any repute would be horrified by this example. Why was our situation different? Because our society, apparently even some professionals who work with

AS kids every day, associates shame with the diagnosis, as illustrated by the example above. While I don't advocate shouting from the rooftops about your child's diagnosis, I would urge you to help destigmatize this diagnosis in ways that make sense to you, your child, and your situation. As the saying goes, change starts at home.

Age-Appropriate Information

If you've decided to share information about his diagnosis with your child, you may be wondering how much is "just right" and when it is a good time to tell him. This topic is hotly debated, so you will need to decide what makes sense in your situation. The first and most important guideline is to listen to your child and find out what worries him about his life and environment. As much as possible, follow your child's lead. If he asks a question, my advice is to tell the truth. Kids have an uncanny way of remembering every-thing we've told them, years later. Your child needs to trust that you will tell him the truth, albeit in ways that don't hurt.

As to when to tell your child about the diagnosis, giving it the name Asperger Syndrome, that's a matter of when it seems right for your child. I told mine at age 8, but for very preco-cious children, earlier might make sense. For other children who may not be able to process this information, middle school might make sense. Remember that your children are watching TV, reading magazines, surfing the Internet, and overhearing your conversations. It's a little like sex, I sup-pose. Would you rather your children got the information from indirect sources or would you rather tell them yourself?

The following pages contain some guidelines that may help you formulate ways to talk to your child about what is hap-pening to him.

Grade Level	What Your Child May Be Aware Of	The Message to Send
Preschool	Testing or assessment	Mom and Dad are meeting with someone who knows lots about kids. We think that they can help us figure out a way to help you (make friends, be able to sit still in class, etc.).
	Lack of friends	Everyone is different, and not everyone has lots of friends. Maybe it's harder for you to make friends. Let's look at what we can do to help you make a few good friends.
	Behavior issues	Some kids have a harder time keeping themselves calm. You might be one of those kids, and that's okay. So let's look at ways we can help you be more successful.
Lower Elementary School	Testing or assessments	Mom and Dad are meeting with someone who knows lots about kids. We think that they can help us figure out a way to help you.
	Lack of friends	Maybe it's harder for you to make friends than some other kids in class. That's okay. Not everyone is as good at (math, Pokémon, etc.) as you are. Let's look at some ways to help you work on making some new friends.
	Behavior issues	It seems to be harder for you to sit still than some other kids, and that's okay. We need to work with your teacher to find ways that work for you so that you can learn to not disrupt the class.

Grade Level	What Your Child May Be Aware Of	The Message to Send
Lower Elementary School (Cont.)	Easily frustrated	Sometimes you get really frustrated when you're working on something, and it feels even worse because you see other kids doing the work easily. Everyone's different. Let's see what we can do to help you get the work done without getting frustrated.
	Poor motor skills	You seem to be upset that you didn't make a homerun in the game today. Not everyone is great at sports, and it's really hard to make a homerun. Let's go outside and practice and see if that helps.
	Obsession with item	I know that you love dinosaurs, and that's okay, but not everyone is as interested in them as you are. When you're talking in class, you need to work on trying to be interested in what other people are talking about and not always talk about dinosaurs, okay?
Upper Elementary School	Testing and assessments	Mom and Dad are sending you to a psychologist who helps kids who have some difficulties at school or at home. We'll be meeting with the doctor, too. If you have any questions for the doctor, let's write them down so we make sure to get answers, okay?

Grade Level	What Your Child May Be Aware Of	The Message to Send
Upper Elementary School (Cont.)	Lack of friends	It's harder for you to make friends because the rules for friendship don't come naturally for you. That's okay; it's not your fault. You can learn these rules, and we'll help you.
	Behavior issues	Because of the way your brain works, it's harder for you to sit still than some other kids, and that's okay. We need to work with your teacher to find ways that work for you so that you can learn and not disrupt the others. We need you to try your best, but remember that we love you no matter what.
	Executive functioning	It's harder for you to keep your school things in order. Let's work with the teacher to come up with a simple system that works for all of us. I'll need your help to make the system work, okay?
	Easily frustrated	I know you get really frustrated when you're working on something difficult, especially when you see other kids doing the work without any problems. That's okay. Everyone's different. Let's see what we can do to help you get the work done without getting as frustrated.

Grade Level	What Your Child May Be Aware Of	The Message to Send
Upper Elementary School (Cont.)	Poor motor skills	You look upset because you didn't make a homerun in the game today. That's okay; not everyone is destined for the Majors. All I ask is that you try your personal best. Let's go outside and practice.
	Obsession with an item	When you're talking in class, work on trying to be interested in what other people are talking about. Please watch for expressions on their faces that tell you they are not interested, and when that happens, make sure to ask them a question about themselves, like we practiced.
	Trouble with processing	Sometimes you have a hard time figuring out what parts of the story you should talk about in your reports, because of the way your brain stores information. I know it's frustrating because it all seems important. Let's work on recognizing what the main themes are in the books we read together and the TV shows we watch, okay?
Junior High or Middle School	Testing and assessment	We're taking you to a psychologist to see if we can understand why some things are harder for you. Although we need to do this as a family, if you would like to talk to the doctor alone about what this all means, that's fine.

Grade Level	What Your Child May Be Aware Of	The Message to Send
Junior High or Middle School (Cont.)	Easily frustrated	I know that you get frustrated easily. I'd like to help you work through this, if I can, so that we can find ways for you to not get so upset, is that okay?
	Executive functioning	It's hard for you to keep all of your homework and schoolwork straight. We need to come up with a system that works for you, and we need a way for you to remember to ask for help in class or after school. Will you help me?
	Obsession with an item	Lots of kids get really involved with one special theme, like you. While it's okay to have this favorite, you need to understand that not everyone wants to hear about it all the time. Try to read other people's faces like we've worked on, and if they are getting bored, please remember to ask them a question about something they like.
	Trouble with processing	I know you don't like writing papers because you think it's hard to sort out the information. Let's review some of the steps to gathering information and see if we can sort it all out together. Or, maybe it's time to get a tutor to help. How would you feel about that?

Grade Level	What Your Child May Be Aware Of	The Message to Send
High School	Testing and assessment	We think we need to get some information from a psychologist about why some things are harder for you. We want you to be an active part of this process, and would like you to think about the questions you want to ask the doctor yourself. We also think it would be a great idea for you to talk to the doctor without us there.
	Easily frustrated	I know that you get frustrated easily – this is probably part of your AS. I'd like to help you work through this, if I can, so that we can find ways for you to not get so upset. Is that okay?
	Obsession with an item	Lots of kids with AS get really involved with one special theme, like you and your favorite topic. While it's okay to have this topic, you need to understand that not everyone wants to hear about it all the time. Try to read other people's faces like we've worked on, and if they are getting bored, please remember to ask them a question about something they like.
	Trouble with processing	I know you don't like writing papers because you think it's hard to sort out the information you're supposed to write about. This is part of your Asperger Syndrome. Let's review some of the steps to gathering information and see if we can sort it all out together. Maybe we can get a tutor to help you instead?

Reframing the Situation to a Teaching Moment

Regardless of what you decide to tell your child, it's important to remember that any disability your child may have is only a small part of who he is. Make sure that he is getting equal (indeed, far greater) attention for all of his "typical" behaviors, abilities, and skills. Emphasize and play to his strengths, while gently helping him to work on his weaknesses.

It's important to use whatever teaching moments present themselves. As mentioned, kids with AS often have problems with empathy. Empathy is one of the continuing topics of conversation in our home. For example, when Will comes home and goes off on some kid who has bothered him at school for asking "dumb questions," I try to reframe this, gently leading him toward a more empathic response. "Remember the time when you were learning how to play baseball and you couldn't keep the rules straight on when you could steal a base? Well, maybe Jimmy is having a hard time remembering his math facts. Not everyone is good at everything. Try to remember how bad it felt when you got teased about stealing second base. Do you think Jimmy feels bad, too, when people tease him about his scores in math?"

This may seem remedial, but as much as we want others to be tolerant with our children, we must work very diligently to teach them tolerance, something that does not come naturally to many of them.

When working with your child, keep in mind that she may not master everything she sets out to do, at least at first. This is doubly hard with kids with AS because they tend to get frustrated easily. So, there are two lessons here. One in perseverance, and the other in learning to find ways that work for your child. There is more information under the Cheap Tricks headings in later chapters about easy ways to help him be successful.

Finally, it's important to remember that your child's diagnosis is not to be used as a way of discounting troubling or troublesome behavior. A diagnosis is an explanation for behavior, not an excuse. You and your child are responsible for doing what you can to make sure that your child is not disruptive or rude to the extent possible.

Current Thinking in the Educational Setting

How AS is viewed and handled in the educational setting varies widely from district to district and from administrator to administrator. Some districts embrace these disorders and have inclusive systems in place to accommodate them. Other districts seem to disbelieve the importance of providing services to these children, and some administrators believe that Asperger Syndrome is the "disease of the week," as I was once told by our district's director of special education. Yet other administrators think that children are being diagnosed with AS who don't really have it, and that they are unnecessarily taxing an already under-funded program.

Additionally, the type of services available to your child will vary from district to district and from school to school, depending on who is overseeing the program at the district level and the amount of sensitivity and experience with AS the service provider has. This is to be expected at this time, as the disorder is relatively new, and there are few quantifiable data about what interventions actually work (though researchers are currently compiling data on this subject).

Because of these variables, it's reasonable to assume that educators may want to keep the label of AS quiet, as most of the educators I worked with did. The focus, they maintained, should be on the child's "mainstream ability"; that is, the fact that my child is "typical" in most ways should be the focus, not his differences. This goes hand in hand with the federal law's requirement[2] to keep all children with disabilities in the least restrictive environment (LRE) and, to a large degree, is a reasonable point of view.

No parents want their child labeled, especially given that school-age kids can be remarkably cruel with name-calling, teasing, shunning, and so forth. And in our culture there is a definite focus on homogeneity – we as a culture don't tolerate differences nearly as well as we'd like to think. So, your school district, like mine, may advise you against telling other children about your child's differences or disclosing this diagnosis to others outside the family.

This is a double-edged sword. No parent wants to make her child the brunt of bullying, teasing, and name-calling. Nor does she want her child to not strive to be the best he can be, regardless of a diagnosis. Kids with AS are generally mainstreamed, and are generally able to reach productive lives with the help of early intervention. But without some sort of sensitivity training of his or her peers, the AS child will often suffer the labels of "geek," "nerd," or "weirdo." Is this any better than the label Asperger Syndrome? At least with the diagnosis out in the open, there is an explanation, other than general bratty and geeky behavior, for the child's sometimes-odd behavior.

---

2.   The Individuals with Disabilities Education Act (IDEA) (P.L. 101-476; reauthorized in 1997, P.L. 105-17; 20 U.S.C. 1400 et seq.).

Name-calling hurts. Being bullied hurts. Being ostracized hurts. While I don't advocate full disclosure to all peers in all circumstances, school districts and parents owe it to their children to ensure that they are appropriately supporting the child with AS. This may mean that the parents selectively tell a few other parents whom they believe are sympathetic. It may also mean that the school provides an educational program to all students on disability sensitivity. In some cases, this may mean that a classroom must be told, in age-appropriate language and with extreme sensitivity, about a fellow-classmate's difficulty, so that the children can begin to understand, and hence empathize, with this child's plight.

If you take the "let's get it out in the open" approach, expect to meet resistance along the way. You may wish to retain an educational advocate who can help you make the case to the educators at your child's school.

Remember, You Get to Decide

The long and the short of it is, you get to decide what your child knows, when, and in what context. I don't advocate telling a child more than he needs to know at a given time, nor do I advocate telling a child all the intricate details about the disorder. What I do advocate is to share with your child, as appropriate, why he has problems in some areas and to focus on his strengths, as well as to encourage your child to believe that any areas of weakness can be overcome with help.

One way to frame this is to look at other children's areas of weakness. Not all children are good at math, not all children are good at sports, not all children are good at being kind and thoughtful, and not all children are good at making friends. We all have areas in which we excel. Make sure your child gets plenty of strokes for what he does well. Then, slowly and with great compassion, help him understand and begin to overcome the areas he needs to work on.

Most important, make sure your child understands that you love him just the way he is, unconditionally. This is the best gift you can give any child, regardless of ability.

Chapter 3

Your Team of Experts

From the minute you get a diagnosis of Asperger Syndrome or a related disorder, a team of experts automatically starts to assemble, who will help support your child. Some of these people will be part of your child's school program; others may be sought out as the need arises. Each person brings a specific set of skills with which to help your child.

Following is a brief discussion of each type of expert, intended to help you determine whom to turn to at any given juncture. Where applicable, I have included information about credentials for each expert, as well as how to locate a specialist, if you have the need.

Diagnostician

Diagnosticians can take many forms. It can be someone from the school district, or someone you hired independently. She can be a psychologist or a psychiatrist with a specialty in what is called early-onset disorders, into which the autism spectrum disorders fall. Your diagnostician is a key ally in that his or her professional opinion will be the basis on which school-funded interventions are likely to be founded.

What the Diagnostician Can Do to Help

Beyond giving you a clear diagnosis (that's the hope at least), your diagnostician should able to provide you with referrals and resources to help you set the wheels in motion to get interventions (buzz word for help) for your child. Intervention recommendations may be referrals to speech and language specialists, therapy groups where children learn social skills (often called Friend's Clubs), or general advice on how to request that an IEP be started for your child.

Sometimes, diagnosticians can be of direct service and may provide therapeutic interventions themselves. At other times, diagnosticians only provide diagnoses. Regardless, they should be able to provide you with a map of which roads to take next, given your child's specific needs and strengths. Any information your diagnostician gives you is worth following up on, as he or she is often in a unique position to know what services will best benefit your child.

When to Turn to a Diagnostician

Beyond your child's initial diagnosis, you may need the diagnostician's services again in the future if diagnosis is called into question, such as during a triennial review of your child's IEP. Further, I've found it useful to stay in touch with our diagnostician (a clinical psychologist) from time to time to see what new ideas, leads, or special interventions she has learned in the intervening years.

Pediatrician

In most of the literature I read about AS early on, authors recommended contacting the child's pediatrician in order to get leads on services in the area, as well as recommendations for treatment.

My own experience has shown that pediatricians are often not the right source for this type of help. Some may know what to do, where to go, and so forth, but I think that they are the exception rather than the rule. After you receive a diagnosis, you should share it with your child's doctor, and if he has good ideas and resources, by all means take them. But by and large, a pediatrician is (and should be) primarily concerned with your child's physical well-being. As AS becomes more mainstream, and as more doctors become cross-functional, pediatricians may have access to more useful information for parents.

In the meantime, use your pediatrician to help keep your kid physically well. You can also ask for a referral to a child psychiatrist if that is what you need, or for referrals to child advocacy agencies in the area. A caveat, however: I personally would not accept a prescription for any drugs to treat AS symptoms from any doctor not specializing in this area. So if your pediatrician offers you a mood-altering drug or a drug for attention deficit, I would ask many questions about his or her work with AS children before giving the drug to my child. Or, I would ask for a referral to a psychiatrist who works with AS or general pervasive development disorders before I agreed to try a drug therapy.

Some kids with AS do very well with ADHD-type drugs such as Ritalin and Concerta, and kids with depression or anxiety may need chemical help as well, but make sure you make the decision based on facts, not emotions or expectations (the doctor's or yours) of a quick fix.

Finally, a note on immunizations. The controversy continues to rage on whether or not immunizations might trigger an already predisposed child to developing one of the disorders on the autism spectrum, including AS. My son had a violent reaction to his first DTP immunization, specifically to the pertussis vaccine, and therefore did not receive additional immunizations for whooping cough. Nevertheless, when my daughter was born, I had her immunized fully. I did so because I knew that as a girl she had a relatively low chance of having AS, but also because as a responsible parent, I had to weigh the known benefits of immunization against the possible negative side-effects. What you choose is up to you. Be a responsible parent, read up, ask questions, and do what's right for your child.

The School District

Your local school district has many trained professionals who will be working with your child. For this reason, you should absolutely consider these professionals part of your team of experts who can help your child.

Director of Special Education

A director of special education (sometimes called student services) oversees the administration of services to children with special needs within a school district. Not all school districts have this position, and districts often call this position by another name. Find out who in your school district is responsible for managing the district's special needs services.

If this position does exist, the director's job is to manage all providers of special education services, such as speech therapists, psychologists, occupational therapists, and special education teachers who only teach children with special needs. Further, this person is responsible for ensuring that the federal law governing IEPs and 504s (a different, but similar education plan for children; see The Oft-Dreaded IEP for more information) is adhered to by all employees and the district as a whole. This means that when you have a problem with your child's educational plan, and you've tried to work it out with the staff at your child's school, the director is your next stop.

The director is also usually responsible for the funds allocated to special education and, therefore, has direct authority in deciding which children get services and which do not. The director decides what special training both general and special education teachers receive. For example, if you have an issue with a speech teacher who knows nothing about AS, speak to the director.

Qualifications
Generally, a director of special education has similar credentials as other educational administrators, such as an MA or PhD in education, or an EdS (educational specialist), and will likely have a focus, either academically or experientially, in special education. Every state, and indeed most school districts, has different requirements. There are no state or federal laws governing this position.

Speech Therapist/Pathologist
Speech and language pathologists or therapists assess, diagnose, and treat speech, language, cognitive, and other communication-related disorders. In the context of a child with AS, speech teachers often administer what's called speech

pragmatics therapy. Speech pragmatics is the system of communication, both verbal and nonverbal, and includes maintaining eye gaze, taking turns in conversations, reading and giving facial expressions, and learning other nonverbal social cues (like telling that someone is bored with your conversation if he turns away with a glazed look in his eyes). Additionally, a skilled speech teacher will teach about inference (guessing the meaning of a word or saying, including humor), as well as more general social skills. Finally, this person may also teach study habits and executive functioning skills (such as how to keep your binder organized).

Speech teachers with an MA degree administer diagnostic oral and written tests related to speech deficits. If the teacher has been hired by the district, he or she will relay the test findings to the IEP team, including you as parents (see The Oft-Dreaded IEP for more information about this process). Your child's speech teacher will work with you either directly or you as part of the IEP team to tailor a plan for your child to improve his deficit, and will probably retest your child every three years as part of the triennial evaluation in speech and pragmatics.

Speech teachers provide direct services to your child, and will likely work with your child's teachers and other specialists on a comprehensive plan. This may mean that the speech teacher works with the child in the classroom, though many general education teachers find this distracting to the rest of the class. If this is the case, the speech teacher will provide pullout interventions, where the child goes to another classroom for services.

Qualifications
Nearly all states (45 out of 50) regulate licensing of speech teachers, and most require an MA, a national examination, and postgraduate clinical work in a supervised setting.

Speech teachers can also become certified in CCC-SLP (the Certificate of Clinical Competence in Speech-Language Pathology), which requires an MA, 375 hours of supervised clinical work, a formal fellowship, and a written examination.

Finding a Speech Therapist/Pathologist

There may be times when the district does not believe that your child needs speech therapy and you decide to secure these services for your child independently, at your own expense. Getting your child help is vital, so hire one if you need to. Even if your child does receive speech therapy at school, you may also wish to augment your child's intervention with a private speech teacher. For more information on speech-language pathologists, contact:

American Speech-Language-Hearing Association
    10801 Rockville Pike, Rockville, MD 20852
    http://professional.asha.org

School Psychologist

Not all school districts have a psychologist on staff, but they should have an independent psychologist on retainer whom they regularly use to work with students having difficulty of one sort or another. Psychologists are trained in the workings of the mind and human behavior. School psychologists are qualified to administer behavior assessments and intelligence tests. These tests will likely be administered to your child at the first assessment when the district determines whether your child is qualified for special education services, and again at each re-qualifying assessment, every three years. Psychologists also help students overcome learning and behavior problems, and often work with parents, teachers, and other school personnel to provide an appropriate intervention for the child.

In the context of a child with AS, school psychologists will likely work on behavioral issues (impulsivity, acting out, internalizing problems) and may also help with interventions designed to help your child organize his work and time more efficiently. The school psychologist may also be responsible for teaching your child social skills, logical consequences, and other interpersonal and logic-based skills.

Qualifications

Psychologists have at least an MA in psychology and often have a PhD. Additionally, an EdS (educational specialist) degree qualifies a person to work as a school psychologist. Each of these degrees must be complemented by supervised internship of varying length (depending on type of degree and licensing state). State licensing examinations are required to qualify as a licensed psychologist. Psychologists may be certified by the ABPP (American Board of Professional Psychology).

Finding a Psychologist

Many parents of kids with AS take their children for therapies and other services to private practitioners beyond the services they receive in school. To find a psychologist who works with children with AS, you may want to speak to your pediatrician or call a local health services agency for leads. Parents' groups and word of mouth are also excellent sources.

For more information on psychologists and their qualifications, contact:

American Psychological Association
Research Office and Education in Psychology and Accreditation Offices
750 1st St. NE., Washington, DC 20002
http://www.apa.org

School Counselor

School districts may hire a variety of professionals to help students. Nearly all school districts either retain a full-time psychologist (as described above) or counselor, or have access to one on a retainer basis. Unlike psychologists, who must have at least a master's degree, school counselors may not have an advanced degree, and in different districts and at different grade levels may have different specialities, such as elementary (general) counselors, mental health counselors, vocational counselors, and so forth. Check with your district to see what the focus is for the counselor at your school.

In elementary school, counselors generally help children with AS learn basic classroom and playground skills and work with classroom teachers and other professionals to develop an intervention plan that will work for your child. Counselors often work with the teachers, child, and parents to help the child develop good study habits that will benefit him through his academic career. Counselors may also meet with parents to develop strategies that may help the child at home and during transition time between home and school.

In secondary and high schools, counselors' roles often change focus, in that they help a broader range of students plan realistic academic and career goals and may administer vocational testing and operate career centers and career education programs. Students with AS will benefit from these services as they begin to plan their adult lives.

Qualifications

While requirements vary, credentialing may be needed, and all school counselors must pass a state certification examination. About half of school counselors in the United States have MA degrees (many states require an MA). Most states require up to five years of teaching experience before granting state certification.

Additionally, counselors may be voluntarily certified by the NBCC (National Board for Certified Counselors), which earns them the title of National Certified Counselor. This program requires an MA degree or higher from an accredited college or university, two years of supervised field experience, two professional endorsements, and successful completion of the NBCC's licensure examination.

Occupational Therapist

Not all school districts have an occupational therapist (OT) on staff, but most have one or more on retainer to help children with special needs. The occupational therapist's role is to help children with functional disabilities perform tasks necessary in their daily lives.

In an elementary school, this might mean helping a child with AS with motor skills in physical education, helping a child with handwriting problems, or increasing dexterity and muscle tone. OTs may also help your child with computer keyboarding, hand-eye coordination, and visual acuity, depending on what your child's needs are. Some OTs help children with abstract reasoning, decision making, and problem solving, though these skills are often taught by a school counselor or speech therapist.

An OT may recommend specific classroom modifications or tools to help your child through his day. These may include what are called sensory integration therapies, such as the use of special pencils or pencil grips, the use of special mats to sit on (called proprioceptive mats) that help keep the child sitting upright and alert, slant boards to help your child write more easily, and so forth. An OT may also work with your child outside on the playground, building strength, endurance, and coordination in such activities as ball play and rope jumping.

Qualifications

All OTs must have at least a BA or BS degree in occupational therapy from an accredited program, and must be licensed by passing a national certification examination. Some OTs have a master's degree in occupational therapy.

Finding an Occupational Therapist

Parents often fill in the gaps at one point or another in their child's development by hiring an OT to work on specific skills. Word of mouth and contacts at your child's school are the best bets for finding a good OT, as this is a very specialized line of work. For more information contact:

The American Occupational Therapy Association
> 4720 Montgomery Ln., P.O. Box 31220
> Bethesda, MD 20824-1220
> http://www.aota.org

Physical Therapist

Not all school districts have a physical therapist (PT) on salary, but they should have access to one for children who need them. Like OTs, PTs work with people to help them gain functional improvement in their physical lives. Whereas an OT is primarily concerned with life skills, such as hand-eye coordination, handwriting, and body posture (some of which fall into the category of fine-motor skills), PTs generally work on what are termed gross-motor skills, such as balance, gait, and general muscle tone.

There is overlap between the two professions, especially among those who work with children with special needs.

As a result, some PTs do more fine-motor work, and many OTs do gross-motor work along with the fine-motor work and life skills.

PTs can help AS kids resolve moderate to severe muscle tone problems and issues with general gross-motor skills. Intervention plans may include game playing, endurance training, and learning how to play basic sports and playground games so that the child can be included in regular P.E. and recess activities.

Qualifications

PTs must graduate with at least a BA or BS degree from an accredited program in physical therapy, which includes supervised clinical experience and then pass a state licensing examination.

Finding a Physical Therapist

Like OTs, PTs may be retained by parents who feel that their children will benefit from the extra help. Word of mouth and referrals from your school district are excellent sources for leads. For more information, contact:

American Physical Therapy Association
    1111 North Fairfax St.
    Alexandria, VA 22314-1488
    http://www.apta.org

Classroom Aides

Some districts or schools employ classroom aides to help children with special needs through their school day. Aides may be assigned to just one child for all or part of the day or may work with several children in the same class. Other names for this position include paraeducators, teaching assistants, classroom assistants, and learning support assistants.

Classroom aides are especially helpful if your child is having a rough time in class, either sitting still or getting the proper materials out of his desk in time to keep up with an assignment. Aides can also help during transition times, moving from one station to another or from the classroom to the playground.

Whether or not your child has an aide in the classroom is generally decided as part of the IEP process. Some parents and professionals are concerned that a child only have an aide if really necessary, especially past second or third grade, as the presence of the aide is like a flashing neon sign to the other kids in the classroom that your child isn't able to work independently. If your child needs an aide, advocate to get one. Just be aware of the potential side-effects mentioned above.

Qualifications

There are no formal qualifications for classroom aides. They may be parents who are working at their child's school, students or adults who have an interest in working with children, or undergraduates working toward a degree in psychology, special education, and so on. Regardless of their qualifications, not all aides are created equal. If your child's aide does not understand AS, or how to deal with him on a one-to-one basis, it may not be an effective relationship. On the other hand, you may find an absolute winner with no experience whatsoever who makes a huge difference to your child. Ask questions, and if the relationship is not working out, speak to the person who is administering your child's IEP (see The Oft-Dreaded IEP) about finding someone else to work with your child.

Educational Advocates

Educational advocates (EAs) are retained by parents who are having difficulty securing appropriate services for their child or having trouble with the application or administration of a child's IEP or 504 Plan. Educational advocates are knowledgeable about local and federal law as it applies to services for children with special needs, and often have established relationships with the administrators of local school districts. As such, they can be extremely helpful in situations where you have been unable to secure services for your child by helping you navigate the complex process.

Generally speaking, an EA meets with you to discuss your child's case and what services he might need. While usually not a lawyer, an EA can give you practical advice on what types of services your child might qualify for and then work with the district to secure adequate services.

Educational advocates routinely go with parents to IEP meetings to provide another viewpoint, help you make the points you want, negotiate between you and the district, and give you moral support. IEP meetings can be stressful and overwhelming, and having an EA with you might make a world of difference in presenting your case effectively.

Educational advocates also have a good idea of what is "reasonable" and can give you an honest answer as to what types of services your child should be receiving. While some parents don't know what services their children should be getting, other may insist on services that are not needed, which puts the district on the defensive. A good EA can tell you what you should ask for and what you can reasonably expect.

Finally, EAs can attend fair hearings with you. A fair hearing is a form of mediation used when the district and the parents (or guardians) cannot come to an agreement on how an IEP should be written or executed. More information on this process is found in the chapter The Oft-Dreaded IEP.

Most parents will never need to hire an EA. Most IEPs go fairly smoothly, with all parties working together for the benefit of the child. But when things get sticky, having an EA on your side can be the right choice.

Qualifications

There are no formal qualifications for an EA, but most have significant experience in the educational system and a good understanding of the concepts of a free and appropriate public education (FAPE)[1] and the federal laws governing IEPs. Asking for references is an excellent idea when interviewing an EA, as well as finding out whether the EA has done work before in your school district and how successful he or she was.

The best way to find a good EA is through word of mouth, parent groups, or non-confrontational allies in the school district. The Yellow Pages or the Internet are also good ways of finding an EA:

http://www.a2zeducationaladvocates.com/

http://www.education-a-must.com/

http://www.successadvantage.com/Educational.htm

http://www.advocatesforchildren.org/links.php3

---

1. For more information on free and appropriate public education, refer to http://www.fapeonline.org/.

Lawyer

You can probably surmise why lawyers are mentioned in this section. If you turned to this section first, however, go back and read the rest of this chapter. Hiring a lawyer should be your very last resort after you have explored, with due diligence, all other remedies. For example, I heartily recommend that you work with an educational advocate before you hire an attorney.

Once you hire a lawyer, either to instill fear in the hearts of your school's administrators or to actually file suit, you will have irreparably damaged your relationship with the district and will forever be seen as distrustful or unwilling to work things out reasonably. This does not mean that you should never hire a lawyer. However, you should know that if it is your first response to a lackluster or inappropriate IEP outcome, people will say fairly, including court judges, that you failed to work the system as it is intended.

Qualifications

All lawyers must graduate from an accredited law program and pass the national and state bar examinations to practice law.

Finding a Lawyer

Probably the best way to find a lawyer who specializes in this area is from an EA (and remember, you should have already worked with an EA to get to this point). Word of mouth and parent groups are good sources of leads, as well as looking in the Yellow Pages or on the Internet.

Information on law schools and a career in law may be obtained from:

American Bar Association
    750 North Lake Shore Dr.
    Chicago, IL 60611
    http://www.abanet.org

Parent Groups

Being the parent of a child with AS can make you feel like an alien. Compared to the skills of other parents, yours often seem ineffective. What appears to come naturally to other parent-child relationships may be difficult in yours. Further, having an AS child can be downright frightening and overwhelming at times. Managing the practical and legal aspects of an IEP, figuring out how to overcome your child's fears and dislikes, and facing the very real adjustment to the fact that your child is somewhat different can tax even the strongest individual.

You are not alone. There are lots of other parents out there who are facing the same challenges. Some have more experience than you, some have less, but nearly all of them will have something to share that can help you through this. For reasons both practical and supportive, I urge you to find other parents who are facing the same challenge.

Finding a good support group will put you in touch with individuals who have resources you may not have found yet. For example, this is a great way to find out what educational advocates in your area specialize in this field. Talking with parents will help you learn what has worked for them, what hasn't worked, which OTs were great, and which ones were not. Some parents can tell you their experiences, positive and negative, with different school districts and administrators. Further, finding parents of other kids with AS might mean finding a friend for your child.

Finding a Parent Group

If you live in a metropolitan area, there is a good chance that a local hospital or health clinic offers "Friend's Clubs" for children with AS or parents' classes for dealing with these issues. I recommend attending one of these parenting classes, and asking other parents what support groups they know about. Additionally, school districts often host monthly or bimonthly coffee groups for parents of children with special needs. Contact your school district for more information.

There are many regional groups that offer support for AS parents. For a fairly comprehensive listing of support groups throughout the country, check The Source's webpage at http://www.asperger.org/.

Mentors, Tutors, and Coaches

There may be times in your child's life when he might need an older friend to help improve or enhance social skills, work through difficulties in school or sports, or just bolster his self-esteem. If your child is failing to thrive in an area, and you've tried everything you can think of to help, consider finding a mentor, tutor, or coach.

A mentor can be just about anyone, but I recommend a patient teenager or older adult, preferably of the same sex as your child. Mentors can help with homework or after-school activities, or might be able to help a child in the classroom much like an aide. In short, they can provide one-on-one attention in an area where your child has difficulty.

Will has had two mentors in his life, both with huge success. The first was when he was in preschool and was having a really difficult time just getting through the day. He was defiant, wouldn't sit still, wouldn't interact in group settings, and wouldn't follow instructions. The teachers, kind as they were, were frazzled in trying to herd all the other children and then spend special time with Will, coaxing him to comply. First I tried to help, but my presence at the preschool only made things worse – if I was there, Will would simply play with me, and ignore everyone else. He'd cling to me tenaciously, and no patterns of behavior were changing.

I decided to put a sign up at the local universities and colleges advertising for an assistant to "shadow" Will through his day. We found Elliott (after careful interviewing and background checking), a young man just finishing his undergraduate degree in psychology. Elliott went to Will's preschool three times a week and helped him navigate the world of preschool. It worked like a charm. Will got the support he needed, and with gentle reinforcement, Elliott got him to follow the rules. Ten years later, Will still remembers Elliott with great fondness.

A coach can do the same type of thing, although more often on a given skill or problem. For example, if your child is playing a sport, or wants to play a sport, but is having difficulty learning the rules or mastering the motor skills necessary to play, find a parent or teenager who is patient with and likes children, and have the person work on these skills with your child.

Finally, a tutor is useful when your child has a measurable cognitive gap in a given area. While you won't need to hire a tutor every time your child struggles with a new concept or a given subject, if there is an ongoing problem with a single subject, it may be worth hiring a tutor. You can, and should, help your child first at home, but my experience is that children often learn better from others.

Why Parents Shouldn't Try to Be Mentors, Tutors, and Coaches

Your role as a parent is often one of being a mentor and tutor and a coach as well as many other models. I'm not suggesting that those roles are not important for you to play. However, there are some key benefits in finding someone else to work with your child that you may want to consider.

First, you may not be the best person to teach your child a new skill. I couldn't teach my son to play soccer if my life depended on it, but he wanted to play, and because he was unable to learn the game the way other kids did, by watching and jumping in and learning on the job, he had to be instructed, one on one, by someone very patient. A mom I know who plays just about every sport was very willing to teach Will enough of the game so that he could play on a team. Will loved the attention he got from this lovely woman, learned a lot, and was far less resistant to her instruction than he would have been to mine.

Second, because children with AS often don't have a lot of friends, yet seem to have an uncanny affinity for adults, having a mentor or coach work with your child gives him positive reinforcement socially, something he needs from others.

Third, it's important that you be a parent and not a teacher, mentor, or coach all of the time. If most of your time with your child is spent in training on one skill or another, you're missing out on plain old parenting, and your child may feel like he's not good enough in your eyes and that your love for him is only conditional on his mastering some new skill. Let someone else take part of that burden. It will be better for both you and your child. It truly does take a village to raise a child with AS.

Finding a Coach, Mentor, or Tutor
Probably the best way to find a coach or mentor is by word of mouth or hanging out at your child's school. For coaches, find the parents who are mellow and not overly interested in zealous competition, and simply ask them if you can pay them to work with your child for a few sessions. If they don't like the idea of being paid, consider buying them a gift certificate for a local pizzeria or family restaurant in lieu of payment. A kind parent with time to spare will

gladly help your child. Wouldn't you? You can also contact local sports organizations. Explain that you have a child who wants to play, but needs some individual instruction, and ask if they know anyone who might help.

For mentors, I also suggest creating a bulletin with tear-offs at the bottom with your phone numbers. Send a few copies to local colleges and universities that offer undergraduate or graduate programs in social work or psychology. Send them directly to the dean, and ask him or her to post them on job boards. You can also contact the YMCA and other youth organizations in your area to find a suitable person to work with your child.

For tutors, I recommend talking to other parents and to the school staff, who often have knowledge of who is working in the area and might be a good match for your child. If you live in a metropolitan area, look for the free, local parent magazines available at doctor offices and daycare centers for advertisements for tutors.

A Word of Caution

While I firmly believe that 99.99% of the human race is good, there are those who prey on children. If you hire someone to work with your child, do your due diligence and ask for references. For someone under 25, I would ask to speak to his or her parents as well as someone at the college or organization who has known the person for a few years. Follow your instincts. If you think something is "not okay" with someone, don't give him or her access to your child. And make sure you speak to your child regularly about his relationship with a coach, tutor, or mentor, to make sure that nothing untoward is happening in that relationship.

Chapter 3

You (The Sermon)

This is probably the most important part of this book, so get ready. It's a subject I'm very vocal on, because it makes all the difference in the world to your child.

Regardless of his strengths or weaknesses, you are your child's best advocate. Period. End of story. If you are expecting someone else to ride in on a white horse and do all the hard work and fix everything, wake up. That dream is over.

You must advocate for your child. No one else, no one, will do it for you. And if you leave it up to the school districts, the teachers, the psychologists, your parents, or the child himself (at least when he's young), your child will not succeed nearly as well as if you had done the work.

All parents' jobs are to raise their children to be self-sufficient, responsible, and productive adults. Your job is harder because your child has some areas that need extra attention. It is your job to make sure that your child gets the help he needs. Everyone else in your child's life is a supporting actor. Your child is the star. You are the director and producer.

If you have to ship your other children off to gramma's house so you can have a special dinosaur-themed play extravaganza for all the first-grade boys to help your son make friends, do it. If you have to help your child practice his cursive letter G a hundred times, be glad to help. She needs you. And your work will pay off by some day having a grown child who can live a happy and rewarding life. Intervention, especially in young children, makes a huge difference. Keep at it – it does get better, and it does get easier. You will see the difference in time.

The Hysterical Mom vs. the Uninvolved Mom

Parents know how hard it is to tell if they are helping their children or hurting them by being involved with their lives. This is especially true of parents of AS kids. On the one hand, you want to help your child and give her the extra instruction she needs. On the other hand, you want to give her enough room to learn and grow into a self-sufficient person.

Particularly in the educational setting, I've been alternately accused, gently or indirectly, of being both a Hysterical Mom and an Uninvolved Mom. And I'm sure that at times, I may have at least appeared to be both.

The Hysterical Mom is the bane of all educators' existence. We are the ones clamoring for some weird, new therapy for our kids. We are the ones insisting that our kids get a break during a long test to go out on the swings. We are the ones who repeatedly ask for preferential seating in the classroom so that our kids pay attention. In short, we are always asking for additional resources or energy for our kids. To the classroom teacher who has 30 students in her class, to the speech pathologist who cycles through 100 kids a week, we can be a royal pain. Please remember this when you are dealing with your kid's allies in the school district.

Your child is only one in a legion of kids, all of whom have some sort of special need. Also be aware that some well-meaning (and some not-so-well-meaning) educators may try to convince you that little Tommy really doesn't need all that extra attention, that you're being overprotective. And maybe you are. You have to go with your gut on these issues. For example, will your child get significant benefit from a special resource or instructive aide? If you feel strongly enough about something, err on the side of being labeled a Hysterical Mom. Be aware, though, that you need to pick your battles. Fight for the things that are truly important and let the rest go. Also, it's important that the school see you as an ally, willing to bake cupcakes, help in the computer lab, donate books, whatever you can do. Be a provider of special services as well as a consumer, and most educators will smile beneficently on you and your child.

The Uninvolved Mom is less annoying to the educator by and large, but can be equally frustrating. Uninvolved Moms allow their children to fail their spelling tests because they refuse to sit still to study. We are the ones who stopped coming to class to read books because our children were clinging to us to the point of distraction. We are the ones who forget to remind our children for the billionth time that a big report is due and needs to be finished tonight. Just like all other kids, kids with AS need to learn some hard lessons about consequences. This doesn't mean you shouldn't work with your children to motivate them, create a good environment for them to study in, and give them access to resources, but occasionally you will need to use consequences when all else seems to fail.

Sometimes you have to let go and let your kid fall flat on his face. However, while the plan is for this strategy to help teach hard lessons, be prepared to have some people call you uninvolved. The best offense is a good defense, and if you feel you need to let go at some point, contact your child's teachers as soon as possible. Also note that some educators and psychologists may try to cite your lack of involvement as further hindering your child. Listen to your instincts. If you are truly indifferent to how your child is doing in school, then you need to be more involved.

I've been called both uninvolved and hysterical or overinvolved, sometimes in the same school year, sometimes by the same teacher, and yes, once, in the same discussion! That's okay. Your child's teachers know what's going on in class, but they may not be aware of all the dynamics on the playground, in the lunch line, at home, with friends, with family, and so forth. You see your child like no one else does – holistically, and hopefully, evenhandedly. Use your own best judgment for each situation, and try not to worry about what other people think.

Get Smart, Read up, and Take Classes

One of the most important aspects of being your child's advocate is to become as smart as you can by reading, taking parenting classes (especially those for parents of kids with special needs), and joining parent groups for parents of special needs kids. There is a wealth of information out there, from websites, advocacy groups, and scientific journals. Read it all. Learn it all. Your knowledge on the subject will pay off, by keeping you up to date on new therapies, new laws, and new techniques for parenting.

The reference section at the end of this book includes many resources to check out. I also recommend looking for a local parents' group that you can join. Aligning yourself with other parents who have similarly challenged children will open up a world of help to you, most important, support and references to local experts.

If you do find local experts in the field, and if they offer seminars or classes for educators, see if you can attend one of them. Finally, take the time to read general parenting books, such as *How to Talk So Your Kids Will Listen & How to Listen So Your Kids Will Talk* by Adele Faber and Elaine Mazlish (1999), and *Good Friends Are Hard to Find* by Fred Frankel and Barry Wetmore (1996), as well as attend any general parenting classes you can find. Every little bit helps.

Take Care of Yourself

There will be times when the stress becomes overwhelming. This is true for any parent, but particularly so if you are dealing with a child with special needs. Your child can only be as well adjusted and happy as you are. And if your world is falling apart, you need to look for solutions.

If you feel like you're unraveling, and you haven't looked into a parent's group, start now. Because there is still some stigma attached to Asperger Syndrome, you may find yourself unable to talk to friends and family about your child's special challenges. Find people who understand. Just being able to talk helps.

If things are really stressful, you may want to consider therapy, either for yourself or for the family. Having a kind, nonjudgemental ear to dump on can be a very useful way to unburden yourself from the sometimes heartbreaking task of raising a child with AS. Further, a good professional can offer ideas on how to cope and can help you watch out for symptoms, such as depression.

Taking care of your children is important, but taking care of yourself is important, too. Don't forget hot baths, brisk walks, cheesy novels, afternoon naps, and an occasional chocolate binge – whatever works for you.

Lighten Up!

Maybe one of the hardest things to remember, especially if you're in a pitched battle with a school district or having to cope with daily meltdowns at dinnertime, is to lighten up. No matter what diagnosis your child has, she should have ample opportunity to just be a kid even though she has important business to do in school and socially.

Being a kid may look a little different to your child. This means that your interaction with your child may have to be a bit modified. Instead of going out and playing catch, your child may opt to have you memorize all 500 Pokémon. Annoying as this may be, if your kid thrives on Pokémon, dinosaurs, refrigerators, or flannel stories, let him feast on it once in a while. Yes, it's important to help your child learn reciprocity and entertain interests other than his most favorite, but it's not wise to never let him indulge in the things that are really important to him.

A surefire way to connect with your child is to try to share this hobby or interest, no matter how overzealous it may be. Why? Because it shows respect for your child and his feelings and interests. He has to listen to your tales of getting the bubblegum out of his shirt, his sister's hour-long dissertation on the difference between Crayola markers and RoseArt markers, so make sure you give him room to be himself.

And laugh! While it's never a good idea to tease your child about his deficits, it doesn't mean that everything about his deficits are unfunny. When Will was a dino-maniac, we made up a game called "I'm Thinking About a Dinosaur." Someone would select a letter of the alphabet, and then each person would think of a dinosaur that started with that letter. The object of the game was to guess each other's dinosaur, so the idea was to come up with the most obscure dinosaur you could think of.

When he was older, I once bet my son a dollar that he couldn't go a whole day without saying the word "Poké-mon." It was hysterical. He caught himself repeatedly, used other ways to describe these beasts, and tested every limit he could by saying, "Pokeys," "Pocket Monsters," and "Mon-Mons." At the end of the day, I owed him the dollar, and we had not only created a warm memory, but he learned, in a fun and lighthearted way, how pervasive his love of Pokémon was.

References

Faber, A., & Mazlish, E. (1999). *How to talk so kids will listen & how to listen so kids will talk.* New York: Avon Books.

Frankel, F., & Wetmore, B. (1996). *Good friends are hard to find.* Los Angeles: Perspective Publishing.

Chapter 4

The Oft-Dreaded IEP
Part 1 – Getting to Yes

It's time to jump into IEPs. An IEP (individualized education program) is a legal contract that you and the school district enter into to ensure that your child benefits appropriately from his education. All districts must provide you with information on IEPs if you request it, but the process can be bewildering, if not downright intimidating. This chapter will help dispel some of the fear of the unknown.

The Law – A Primer

This chapter gives an overview on how IEPs work, but I heartily recommend reading more on this subject so that you learn all of the nuances of the legal code. Particularly helpful books are *Hopes and Dreams: An IEP Guide for Parents of Children with Autism Spectrum Disorders* by Kirby Lentz (2004) and *The Complete IEP Guide* by Lawrence M. Siegel (1999). In the meantime, let's get our feet wet.

What Your Child Is Entitled to Under Federal Law

Specific federal laws govern the inception, process, and execution of the IEP. IEPs fall under the Individuals with Disabilities Education Act (IDEA), which guarantees that children with disabilities are appropriately served in public schools. All children are entitled to a "free and appropriate public education" (often referred to as FAPE), and children who qualify for an IEP are guaranteed access to an education that is designed to meet their special needs. This guarantee starts when the child is 3 years old, and if you have an early diagnosis, your child can be qualified for help in preschool. Contact your local school district for information.

All school districts are required to follow due process with regard to IEPs and provide special services and modified instruction for children with mental retardation, hearing impairment, speech and language difficulties, and so forth. Most (but not all) children who have been diagnosed with AS qualify for an IEP, either under speech and language deficits or under autism (if your child is severely affected, refer to How Your Child Qualifies later in this chapter).

Note that a school district can put any child on an IEP with the parent's consent even if a formal diagnosis of AS or nonverbal learning disabilities (NLD) is absent. So while the district is legally mandated to make these services available to those who qualify through the traditional methods of testing, assessment, and observation, it can make special services available to anyone it sees fit.

So, why do I call it the "dreaded" IEP? It sounds pretty straightforward so far. I dub it "dreaded" because it's bureaucratic. It's emotionally charged. It's legal mumbo-jumbo. And sadly, it's occasionally worthless in guaranteeing that a child receives the services that she needs. But without it, most children would not get any services.

Your Parental Rights

As a parent (or legal guardian), you have specific rights with regard to the child's IEP. Specifically, you have these rights:

- ❏ You have the right to have your and your child's privacy guaranteed. Other than the school staff, no one has the right to access your child's IEP.

- ❏ You and your child have a legal right that FAPE is met, and that if your child meets the criteria, he will receive special accommodations based on his disability.

- ❏ Once an IEP is in place, you can request an interim IEP meeting at any time. (Regular IEP meetings happen once a year.)

- ❏ You have the right to review your child's school records, and have the right to request that any incorrect or misleading information in these records be amended.

- ❏ You have the right to request additional assessment of your child at any time and for any type of potential deficit, including or beyond that which originally qualified your child for the IEP.

- ❏ You have the right to file a formal complaint against the district if they are out of compliance (not fulfilling their legal responsibilities) in carrying out your child's IEP.

❏ You have the right to due process if you and the district cannot agree on how to execute your child's IEP, either through mediation or a fair hearing, as described later in this chapter.

❏ You have the right to be given a full list of all of your parental rights by the school district when you request an IEP assessment. If you are not given this list of rights, go to the Department of Education's website and download it (http://www.ed.gov/parents/needs/speced/iepguide/index.html).

Walk Softly But Carry a Big Stick

We're mature adults. We know that even if federal law says that something should be a certain way, it is not always how situations work out. Despite all the laws on the books, it is fairly common for districts to miss a step here and there in the execution of an IEP.

Forms get lost, someone new at the school doesn't know you have the right to access your child's records, and so forth. You will find that most of the errors are just that – forgivable human error. However, if your school district continually falls down on the job, constantly gives you the run-around, or fails in any meaningful way (for instance, failing to respond to your request for an IEP assessment), you may need to play hardball.

Failing to follow the law is known as being "out of compliance," and is cause for you to file a formal complaint. Most districts want to avoid this. It costs time and money to respond to a complaint – probably far more money than it would to create an IEP, administer it, and give your child the services she needs.

It's wise to carry the big stick of knowing how the system is supposed to work, but it is equally wise not to use the stick unless you really need to. Most often, a simple phone call to the administrative office saying, "Gee, I was pretty sure the district had five days to respond to me, according to the law" is enough to get the ball rolling. However, if this approach fails to spur the district into action, know that you have legal recourse at your disposal.

A Note on 504 Plans vs. IEPs

While IEPs are the standard tool used to help younger children with AS in school, some districts and administrators steer you to a 504 Plan (504) instead. Additionally, comprehensive IEPs are sometimes no longer needed as a child matures, and the district may suggest that you move him to a 504 once he reaches middle or high school.

Which intervention is deemed most appropriate for your child will vary depending on your child's needs, and may change over time. Simply stated, an IEP is most appropriate for children who need special instruction and a 504 is most appropriate for children who need reasonable accommodation. For example, a younger child may need speech and language intervention in order to learn basic social skills. He may need to take untimed tests after school to be successful. He may need additional instruction in reading comprehension. These needs point to an IEP as the correct instrument. An older child may need to have a weekly check-in with his teacher to make sure he is on track, may need to have homework counted but not graded, and may need to have homework sent to him once a week via email. In this case, a 504 is all that is needed, as the instruction itself is not changed.

504s are governed by a separate set of laws from IEPs. 504s fall under the Rehabilitation Act – the same set of laws that provide wheelchair access to public buildings, sign language interpreters for the deaf, and so on. In short, these laws ensure that school districts provide access to educational programs for all individuals, and are not nearly as comprehensive in scope as IEPs tend to be.

504s expire after a year, so you will need to request a new 504 each year. This is usually not a big deal, but your child could be disqualified at each grade promotion. In contract, an IEP lasts for three years, and carry from one school district to another. 504s do not. 504s generally include vocational help or college preparation. If your child is on an IEP throughout middle and high school, he will be given an ITP (an Individual Transition Plan) at age 16. Working with you and your child, this plan will be carried out by the school district to plan for your older child's future, be it college, vocational school, or work away from home.

Both IEPs and 504s can benefit children with AS. Which is appropriate depends on the age of your child, her specific needs, and how the district intends to help her.

Starting the Process

There are two ways an IEP is started:

1) You request that the school district begin the IEP process and assessment.

2) Your school district asks for your permission to begin an IEP assessment for your child.

Usually, parents request that the school district open an IEP. This is done by sending a letter to the superintendent (or other identified person; you can call the district office to find out whom to send the letter to) indicating that you believe that your child qualifies for an IEP because of his recent diagnosis (which you already have in your hand) of Asperger Syndrome (or NLD, or whatever). If you don't have a diagnosis, you can still make the request based on your observations and, preferably, the observations of your child's teachers. Send all corroborating information (copies of the diagnosis, observation notes, and so on) with your request.

When you write this letter (see Letter Requesting an Initial IEP Assessment in the Resources & References section), make a copy for your own files. From this point forward, save every piece of documentation that you send to the district or one of its representatives, and everything you receive from them. Also start a binder or journal where you can list all the people you have called, record notes from meetings, and so forth. This record-keeping is critical, as there are specific laws that govern how the process is to work, and if you ever need to prove that the district is out of compliance with the administration of your child's IEP, you will need documentation to prove it.

Once the district has received your request, they have 15 days to respond with an action plan, formally and in writing, to your request. Because such letters occasionally get lost, it's a good idea to make a follow-up phone call to ensure your request made it there. Note who you spoke to when you call.

After you review, sign and return the plan, the school district has 60 days to make their own assessment to determine eligibility for your child, even if you come prepared with overwhelming evidence that your child will qualify. That's okay; make sure that the district gives you specifics on what tests they plan to administer, who will be administering them, and what his or her credentials are (most states have specific guidelines for who can administer these tests). See the section on Assessments for information on what each type of test is used for. Also, you are free to call the person the district has selected and ask questions. Explain that you are new to the IEP thing and want more information on what the process is like, what will take place, who is responsible for what, and so forth.

If you call and find that you have serious doubts about this person's ability (or, if you have heard negative things about him), you can formally challenge the assessment once it has been completed if the assessor finds nothing "wrong" with your child (and thereby unqualified for an IEP). This is done through due process, discussed later in this chapter.

Your Child's School Records

If your child is already attending public school by the time you get a diagnosis and start the IEP process, you would be wise to access your child's school records for information that either supports or counters your assertion that your child should be on an IEP.

Because these children usually have high intelligence and verbal skills, and love to please, your child's teachers may see little wrong with your child other than his "stubborn" behavior. This is not true of all teachers, and now that AS and related syndromes have become better known, teachers are becoming more aware of the nuances of this disorder. But because they may not see your child holistically, teachers and other educators may think that you are a Hysterical Mom ranting about special services when all your child needs, according them, is more discipline at home. As the DSM-IV states:

> *In school-age children, good verbal abilities may, to some extent, mask the severity of the child's social dysfunction and may also mislead caregivers and teachers – that is, caregivers and teachers may focus on the child's good verbal skills ... [This] ... may also lead teachers and caregivers to erroneously attribute behavioral difficulties to willfulness or stubbornness in the child.[1]*

As your child's parent and best advocate, you need to be watchful. Her inability to cope with the everyday stresses of school and playground may be punished as conscious misbehavior. This is a nasty cycle, where a child is unable to cope, melts down or acts out, and is then punished for her inability to cope. This cycle often leads to internalized shame, depression, or externalized hurt by making the child even more disruptive. Punishment rarely works in these situations. In addition to direct intervention, children need positive behavior modification to overcome their antisocial acts, and your school should be able to provide this type of behavior intervention as part of his IEP.

As noted above, you can request to view your child's school records on the school campus and you can also request a copy of everything in your child's file for your own records. Make this request in writing. For specific laws and guidelines on requesting copies of your child's file, refer to *The Complete IEP Guide* by L. M. Siegel in the bibliography in Resources & References.

There are cases where damaging information is kept in your child's file for all of his future teachers to read. Not only

---

1. *The Diagnostic and Statistical Manual of Mental Disorders, Version IV.* (2000). Washington, DC: American Psychiatric Association, p. 82.

can this hurt your child's chance for eligibility, it can hinder him getting the understanding from his teachers that

he needs to be successful in school. You can challenge anything that is in your child's record, and you can also write a rebuttal to be added to his record.

Assessments

It is impossible here to include all of the types of assessments that are used by school districts to determine whether a child needs services, and if so, what kinds of services. This section covers some of the most common assessments that you may run into, as well as a brief overview of the assessment process and your rights.

The District's Assessment

Most likely, if you have started the IEP process, the school district will request an independent assessment, regardless of what assessments you have already had done. While this may seem adversarial and a waste of time, it's the way things are generally done, and you are not being singled out for harsh treatment.

If the district asks for an independent assessment, they must notify you in writing, giving you the types of assessments to be used and who will be administering them. These tests are undertaken at the school district's cost, not yours. Sometimes the tests are given at the school by a psychologist, at other times you will be asked to take your child to an assessor's office. Both ways are appropriate, provided the person administering the test is qualified to do so in your state (see discussion on qualifications in Chapter 3).

Once you get the letter regarding the assessment, review it carefully. Is the district asking for the same type of assessments that you have already procured (for example, sending your child to another psychologist when you already have a diagnosis)? If so, it may be challenging the foundation of your claim for an IEP – that your child has AS. If, however, as more frequently happens, the district is asking for different assessments (such as speech and language assessment, behavioral assessments, and so on), they may be trying to understand whether your child's impairment is clinically significant enough to warrant an IEP. In other words, the district may not be challenging the diagnosis, but challenging that your child needs extra help. Or, it may not be challenging anything, just trying to find out where exactly your child's deficits lie and what interventions will be appropriate.

If the plan seems reasonable, by all means accept it. However, if you question the rationale behind the types of assessments the district is asking for, or have doubts about the expertise of the assessor, you do not have to accept the plan. If you don't accept the plan, write a letter explaining why you think the district's approach is inappropriate, and request the type of assessment you think is more fitting. You can also ask that the district add or change the plan, and still accept the initial plan.

When ready, set up an appointment for the assessment, explain to your child that his school wants him to have some additional tests to figure out how best to help him, and go through with the assessment. Make sure that you ask the assessor to mail you a copy of his report when completed.

You have the legal right to the report, and should read it carefully before the IEP meeting. If you do not have sufficient time to read it before the meeting, for example, if the district hands you a copy of the report at the meeting, you may wish to cancel and reschedule the meeting so that you have time to go over the report at your leisure. If you have any questions about the report, contact the assessor with your questions, and make a note of his or her answers in your journal.

If the assessor's report matches what you believe is true for your child, you've got it made, because it is unlikely (though possible) that the district will go against the advice of their hand-picked assessor. If, however, the assessor asserts that your child doesn't need any help whatsoever, you can challenge it. If you have not yet had an independent assessment, get one now. If you have had one done, and your assessment disagrees with the district's, you can use the due process method to challenge (see Requesting Due Process).

Overview of Commonly Used Tests

This section gives an overview of some of the most common tests administered to children in the United States, though tests used vary widely from district to district. Where applicable, relative pros and cons of each test are given.

All formal assessments such as those listed below can only be administered by a qualified individual. Most often, the person must have an MA degree or higher in order to administer an assessment to your child. The only exceptions are tests related to speech and language, which can only be administered by a credentialed and licensed speech and language pathologist or therapist, and the motor skills tests, which can only be administered by a credentialed and licensed occupational therapist. If the district has someone other than a qualified professional administer one of these tests, the assessment can and should be challenged. Note that Cons are listed only when a negative is known. Most of these tests are very commonly administered, and are useful in the right context.

Intelligence Tests

Intelligence tests measure just that: overall intelligence or IQ. These can be helpful in identifying strengths and weaknesses in your child's intelligence, which in turn can point out any vast discrepancies between areas of intelligence. Note that children with language impairment may score below their actual IQ on a verbal or written IQ test. Therefore, a nonverbal IQ test (such as one that uses puzzles or other manipulatives) may be more appropriate.

Intelligence Tests			
Test Name	**Test Type**	**Ages**	**Pros**
Stanford-Binet Intelligence	Intelligence test	2-23	Commonly used IQ test.
Wechsler Intelligence Scale for Children (WISC-III)	Intelligence test	6-17	Overall intelligence test. Very commonly used.
Wechsler Preschool and Primary Scale of Intelligence (WPPSI-R)	Intelligence test focusing on language and perception	4-6	Commonly used test for preschoolers.
Leiter-R	Nonverbal IQ test	2-21	Nonverbal test designed to distinguish children with ADHD and neurophysical impairments. Measures "fluid" intelligence.

Adaptation and Social Skills Tests

Just as they sound, these tests determine how a child is adapting to his or her living environment, including social skills.

Adaptation and Social Skills Tests			
Test Name	**Test Type**	**Ages**	**Pros**
Social Skills Rating System (SSRS)	Mixed: social skills, problem behaviors, and academic competence	3-18	Quick parent questionnaire; can be used in conjunction with teacher and self-test for older children. Separate scoring for boys and girls.
Vineland Adaptive Behavior Scales (VABS)	Mixed: communication, daily living skills, socialization, motor skills	Birth to Adulthood	Very standard. Provides age equivalents, and comparison of different settings. Very commonly administered.
Behavior Rating Inventory of Executive Functions (BRIEF)	Parent and teacher rating forms for executive functioning	5-18	Very standard. Commonly used with children with pervasive personality disorders such as AS.

Speech and Language Tests

Speech and language tests cover a wide range of subareas, such as vocabulary, expressive and receptive language, expressive writing, reading comprehension, auditory processing, problem solving, abstraction, and inference.

Many kids with AS "ace" some of the more fundamental tests; these children should be administered more complex tests to identify potential problem areas in abstract thinking, inference (guessing from clues), and nonliteral language, which are usually weak areas for kids with AS.

Speech and Language Tests			
Test Name	**Test Type**	**Ages**	**Pros & Cons**
Beery Picture Vocabulary Test	Vocabulary	2.5-40	Part of STEA.
Clinical Evaluation of Language Fundamentals (CELF-3)	Understanding and use of semantics, syntax, auditory memory	6-21	Subtests in expressive and receptive language.
Comprehensive Assessment of Spoken Language (CASL)	Oral language comprehension, expression, and retrieval	6-21	Aged-based norms. Identifies disorders as outlined by IDEA. Gives percentile ranking. Very commonly used. *Cons:* Some AS children do very well on this test. Does not test nonliteral language.
Expressive One-Word Picture Vocabulary Test	Expressive vocabulary	2-12 12-16	*Cons*: Very simplistic; children with AS probably do very well on this test.
Language Processing Test (LPT)	Listening and processing skills, oral responses and organization	5-11	Complex test. *Cons:* Does not test inference or other "problem" areas of AS kids.

Speech and Language Tests *(continued)*			
Test Name	**Test Type**	**Ages**	**Pros & Cons**
Peabody Picture Vocabulary Test (PPVT)	Vocabulary	2-40	Measures both vocabulary and hearing.
Receptive One-Word Picture Vocabulary Test	Receptive vocabulary	3-12 12-16	Provides data on "heard" vocabulary. *Cons*: Does not test auditory processing difficulties.
Test for Auditory Comprehension of Language (TACL)	Auditory processing	3-10	Standard test for auditory processing deficits.
Test of Language Competence (TLC)	High-level language skills including abstraction, inference, figurative language	5-9; 9-19	Very standard; gives percentile ranking, gives subtest and overall scores.
Test of Pragmatic Language (TOPL)	Basic speech pragmatic competence including inference	5-14	Very standard; gives percentile ranking. Very commonly administered. *Cons*: Many AS kids do very well on this test. It is noted on the test itself that this test should be administered as part of a battery of tests.

Speech and Language Tests *(continued)*

Test Name	Test Type	Ages	Pros & Cons
Test of Problem Solving (TOPS)	Use of speech for problem solving, determining solutions, empathizing	6-11	Very standard; gives percentile ranking. Very commonly administered. *Cons*: Many AS kids do very well on this test.
Adolescent Test of Problem Solving (ATOPS)	Use of language for reasoning.	12-17	Gives percentile ranking. Students have to answer open-ended questions. *Cons*: Some AS children may do very well on this test.
Test of Written Language (TOWL)	Vocabulary, spelling, grammar, story construction	8-18	Comprehensive test measuring writing ability.
Utah Test of Language Development	Receptive and expressive language	3-10	Very comprehensive test measuring writing mechanics through story construction.

Motor Skills/Sensory Integration Tests

Motor skills and sensory integration tests are commonly used to establish baselines for an AS child and to note any areas of extreme difficulty. Because these tests are administered most often for children with purely physical handicaps, your child may fall within normal ranges. However, any low scores could point to potential areas for work.

Motor Skills/Sensory Integration Tests			
Test Name	Test Type	Ages	Pros
Developmental Test of Visual-Motor Integration (VMI)	Hand-eye ability, fine-motor skills	3-Adult	Part of STEA; very commonly used as baseline.
Peabody Developmental Motor Scales	Gross- and fine-motor ability	0-7	Tests basic motor functioning.
Sensory Integration and Praxis Test (SIPT)	Sensory integration processes	4-9	A commonly used test. Very complete.
Sensory Profile (W. Dunn)	Sensory processing	0-Adult	Comprehensive profile for identifying type and severity of sensory processing issues.
Test of Visual-Motor Skills (TVMS)	Hand-eye coordination, fine-motor skills	3-13	Comparable to VMI.

Behavioral Tests

The Child Behavior Checklist (CBCL) compares a parent's checklist against a teacher's checklist to help identify a child's areas of presumed weaknesses and strengths.

Behavioral Tests			
Test Name	Test Type	Ages	Pros & Cons
Autism Behavior Checklist (ABC, part of ASIEP-2)	Behaviors specific to autism	n/a	Generally filled out by parents to screen for autism. *Cons*: Does not work well with children with AS.
Child Behavior Checklist (CBCL)	Behaviors	2-18	Helpful in identifying areas that teachers and parents believe need work. Adds normative data for boys and girls in a given age group with or without disabilities.
Minnesota Multiphasic Personality Inventory – Adolescent (MMPI-A)	General behavior	14-18	Used to screen out personality disorders to ascertain level of behavioral dysfunction. *Cons*: Not generally useful for AS unless other diagnoses are suspected. Normed on an institutional population.

Other Tests

These tests cover a wide range of areas, from specifically differentiating between autism spectrum disorders to testing general developmental status.

Other Tests			
Test Name	**Test Type**	**Ages**	**Pros & Cons**
Autism Diagnostic Interview (ADI-R)	Assessment and diagnosis of autism and PPD-NOS.	5-early adulthood	Diagnostic tool correlating to the DSM-IV. Useful for differentiating between autism, Asperger Syndrome, and PDD-NOS.
Autism Diagnostic Observation Schedule (ADOS-G)	Assessment and diagnosis of autism and PPD-NOS.	3-Adult	Useful for pre-verbal or non-verbal persons. Often used in conjunction with ADI-R.
Autism Screening Instrument for Educational Planning (ASIEP-2)	Set of five tests: ABC, Vocal Behavior, Interaction Assessment, Educational Assessment, Prognosis of Learning Rate	1.5-Adult	Comprehensive tests to identify presence and severity of autism. Individual subtests may be used.
Battelle Development Inventory	General developmental areas	0-8	Tests basic development. *Cons*: May not pick up nuances of AS.

Other Tests *(continued)*			
Test Name	**Test Type**	**Ages**	**Pros & Cons**
Standardized Test Educational Assessment (STEA)	Set of six tests: WIAT, KeyMath, VADS, VMI, Beery Picture Vocabulary, Monroe Sherman Paragraph Copying	Various	May be used as a baseline to gather a comprehensive assessment of a child. *Cons*: Some of the individual tests are not the best for AS kids.
Visual Aural Digit Span Test (VADS)	Measures ability to remember numerals	School age	Part of STEA, used to determine memory.
Weschler Individual Achievement Test (WIAT)	Mixed; mathematics, reading, writing, language	5-20	Very standard test given as general assessment. Part of STEA. *Cons*: Not particularly useful in determining AS difficulties.
NEPSY	Mixed; used specifically for testing children with learning disabilities, autism, and other disorders	3-12	Relatively new, a very comprehensive test for autism spectrum testing, including AS. Correlates to WISC-III in three main areas; a good selection for baseline testing of AS children. *Cons*: Some subtests are not the best choices for children under 5.

Observations

Part of any assessment is likely to consist of observations made by the school psychologist, speech and language teacher, and/or an outside expert. Observations are very useful in gathering data that cannot be obtained via testing. For example, a child may know how to use social skills on a written assignment, but be unable to generalize these skills to the real world. Only keen observation can gather this useful component of an assessment.

Length and Frequency of Observation

One of the chief complaints I've heard about observations is how few and short they are. Busy professionals working for the school district often don't have the latitude to take several trips to your child's school, nor do they have hours and hours to spend on just observing your child.

This can be a problem in that your child's behaviors may not manifest when the observer is watching. To do justice to a child, an observer should watch the child at least three times over a couple of weeks, and should observe the child for at least half an hour each time. Far too frequently, an observer watches the child once – for 10-15 minutes. This is not nearly enough to formulate an assessment. The district should offer more observations, give more weight to your observations (and the observations of those who are with your child daily, such as playground supervisors), or give less weight overall to the observation, especially if it does not support the goals you are trying to achieve for your child.

Who Does the Observation

During Will's last triennial review, his speech and language teacher performed "an informal assessment for Asperger's" (sic). When I questioned her credentials to perform this "informal assessment," I was told that she had taken a one-day seminar with a local AS specialist, and that this somehow qualified her to determine Will's level of disorder. Ahem.

A sound, thorough assessment will contain information from your child's teachers, perhaps the principal, and any other professionals who have regular contact with your child. This is fine. All of these people bring a fresh perspective on your child, and this information makes for a well-rounded approach.

However, you should be leery of any observations performed to understand a particular area of claimed weakness that is not performed by a specialist in that area. For example, it's perfectly all right for a teacher to document his observations of how your child does in class, but it would be inappropriate for him to say anything about his fine-motor skills other than that he seemed to be having trouble making his letters or had trouble in drawing. Similarly, it is inappropriate for a speech teacher to make recommendations in an IEP based on her observations about your child's psychological makeup.

Where the Observation Occurs

Another potential pitfall of observations is where they occur. As luck would have it, some of the most difficult times for children with AS are frequently missed in observation: transition time, recess and lunch breaks, and P.E. Most observation happens in the classroom or in the speech teacher's room, where many AS kids do pretty well because these environments are structured.

This is not to say that observation should not occur in the classroom – it should. But you should also ask that the assessment includes observations at line-up time, at recess, at lunch, and during P.E. so that the full spectrum of your child's day is accurately portrayed, including all those icky, unstructured times that cause AS kids so much trouble.

Remember, your child has the legal right to be successful throughout the school day, and the school district has to observe him in all potentially difficult settings.

What to Do If the Results of Assessments Disagree

If you have a diagnosis of Asperger Syndrome from a qualified psychologist, you've already provided the district with your first independent assessment. If the district is challenging that diagnosis, and their independent assessment is from an equally qualified psychologist, you are at a stalemate, and you will need to go to due process to resolve the situation.

For example, if you brought a formal diagnosis from a psychologist to assert your child's AS, the district may respond with a speech and language assessment to prove he doesn't really need services. Your next step, then, is to hire a speech and language assessor to prove that he does. Once you have done that, and presented the (hopefully compelling) findings to the district, they may yield and give your child an IEP.

Further, you have the right to request that the district provide additional assessments, at their cost, for any areas of weakness not addressed by their selected assessments. Your request may include additional tests in the same area, or tests in a different area (such as motor functioning).

Some school districts regularly tell parents that tests are not necessary, and some schools may tell you that you must pay for them yourself. While you should be reasonable in your requests, according to federal law, the district cannot deny independent testing or assessment of your child. Ever.

However, you may have to remind the district that this is your right.

The district may also still assert that their assessment is the correct one and refuse to issue an IEP. If this is the case, you can request due process: either mediation or a fair hearing. See the section Due Process in Chapter 5 for more information.

The Decision

If and when your child has been assessed by an outside party, you will receive both a copy of the assessor's report and the decision by the school district as to whether or not your child has qualified under their guidelines. If the district accepts that your child needs an IEP, they will forego the independent assessment and place her on an IEP. A district cannot deny a child an IEP without at least providing independent assessment.

A "No" Decision

If the school district's independent assessment disproves that your child needs an IEP, you have three options:

1) **Accept the decision.** Just because your child has AS or NLD doesn't mean that he needs special ed. The core criteria are whether or not your child is "successful throughout the school day" (which includes recess, lunch periods, and P.E.). If your child has no major problems in speech and language, cognition, or social interactions in the classroom or on the playground, perhaps this decision is a good one. If, however, the child does have significant deficits in this area, he will need help – whether or not the

school district gives it to him. You can opt for using outside services to help him in his weak areas if you have the financial resources and if this makes sense for your situation, or you can challenge the school district's decision.

2) **Challenge the decision.** If you believe that your child needs intervention, your best course is to challenge the school's decision. You can do this by asking for due process: either mediation or a fair hearing (see Due Process in Chapter 5). Both of these options bring together the parents and their information and specialists along with the school district officials and their information and specialists. You can also hire an attorney for either mediation or a fair hearing. Generally speaking, most parents try mediation before a fair hearing, as it is less costly and time consuming. To request due process, write a letter to the district formally requesting that this process that started. (See the sample letter Letter Requesting Due Process in the Resources & References section.)

3) **Change schools.** The fact is that some school districts are far more open and able to help children with special needs than others. This is probably in part due to economics, but it is also due to personality, style, and cultural and social emphasis. I live in a fairly wealthy area, yet many of the local school districts are very adversarial about providing services for children with AS. In fact, some of the best programs I've heard about are in far less affluent communities in the area.

There are good reasons to change schools. If your child has experienced years of trouble in his current school, moving elsewhere may give him a fresh start without all the baggage. If you do some research (by contacting the local office of education, for example), you might find an ideal school with a program already in place. Further, there are more and more specialized schools that cater to children with special needs, and AS kids in particular. These might be wise choices.

Regardless of how you decide to handle a "no" decision, be mindful that this doesn't mean that your child doesn't need any help. You know best: If she is struggling in any aspect of her life, consider getting help outside the school district, either over and above the services she gets in school or in lieu of those the school refuses to provide. It will likely be one of the best things you ever do for your child.

A "Yes" Decision

If the district agrees that your child qualifies for an IEP, you will receive notification in writing, along with a date to meet and discuss what the IEP should contain. You should also receive a copy of all the assessment documents from the district. If they do not send them to you, request that they do so and keep them in your records. If the date the district selects for the IEP meeting does not work for you, you have the right to request another day and time.

How Your Child Qualifies

If the district has agreed that your child qualifies for an IEP, pay particular attention to how she qualified, as this may play a role in the services she receives, and in how long the lifespan of the IEP is (in the district's eyes, anyway).

Students with AS usually qualify in one of two ways: (a) under speech and language disorders, as these children have a strong deficit in this area; or (b) under autism (some districts refine this further by calling this qualification "autism-like disorders").

While a win is a win, in the best of worlds you would want your child to qualify under autism or autism-like disorders, if that's the term the district uses, rather than use speech and language as the qualifier. The reasons for this are numerous. First, an autism qualification nearly guarantees that your child's IEP will be in effect throughout his school years, thereby eliminating the necessity to do battle with the district every three years to continue the IEP. Second, it helps the school relate to your child as he really is – on the autism spectrum – not as a child who has one or two little quirks that he'll likely outgrow anyway. Asperger Syndrome is a pervasive personality disorder. Kids get much better with good intervention and can go on to lead satisfying and meaningful lives, but they are never "cured." Third, with a qualification under autism, you may be able to secure more appropriate services for your child, rather than slap-dash services that are easy to provide and generalized for a larger population of kids with a variety of deficits. If at all possible, raise the bar to its highest level, and ask for an autism qualification if the district has not given it to your child.

Cheap Tricks
for Organizing Your Information

As you start down the path from diagnosis to beginning the IEP process, you need to keep accurate and complete records of everything that transpires. For those of us who are organizationally challenged, here are a few tips.

✋ Folders

The simplest thing to do is to keep simple manila folders with all of the correspondence, reports, magazine articles, and so forth. If there is a great deal of material, you may want to organize the information by school year or by type, such as doctor reports, test results, school correspondence, progress reports from occupational therapists, and so forth. Not only is it important to have a reference to go back to when checking your child's progress, keeping this information is vital if you should ever end up in a legal battle with a school district.

Don't forget to make copies of everything you send to the district, doctors, and therapists.

Additionally, you may want to keep a personal journal of your child's experiences over time. This is useful when your child is having a particularly difficult time, has begun to exhibit new behaviors, or you are trying new parenting techniques at home. When dealing with a rather pitched battle with our school district in which they claimed there was little wrong with my son, I copied several pages of my journal describing what he told me about his school day for a week, and gave them to the administrator. They clearly described what he was going through, and added weight to my argument in favor of services.

✋ **Email Records**

Keep all email that you receive or send regarding your child's diagnosis, IEP, and progress. If you are not comfortable keeping these records on your computer, print them out and keep them in your child's folder. These documents can be vital in the future.

References

Lentz, K. (2004). *Hopes and dreams: An IEP guide for parents of children with autism spectrum disorders.* Shawnee Mission, KS: Autism Asperger Publishing Company.

Siegel, L. (1999). *The complete IEP guide.* Berkeley, CA: Nolo Press.

U.S. Department of Education. (n.d.). *My child's special needs: A guide to the individualized education program.* Retrieved December 30, 2006, from http://www.ed.gov/parents/needs/speced/iepguide/index.html

Chapter 5

The Oft-Dreaded IEP
Part 2 – The Plan

IEP Goals and Objectives

Once you've cleared all of the hurdles described in Chapter 4 and have gotten the IEP meeting scheduled, your next assignment is to ensure that the goals and objectives set forth in the IEP are what your child needs.

While the team of experts that come to the table from the school district probably have years of experience dealing with IEPs, they may not have years of experience in AS, so it's a good idea to understand how the IEP is decided upon, written, carried out, and measured.

What Services Are Needed?

The formal assessments and diagnostic reports you have gathered so far, along with any information you've received from your child's teachers, are all good sources of information to determine where your child needs help. Because of the wide range of disability associated with AS, your child may need minimum intervention, or a great deal of intervention. The following is a breakdown of typical interventions and services.

- ❏ **Speech-Language Therapy**
  Speech-language therapy covers a broad range of deficits, from articulation (which some children may have problems with on top of their AS) to language processing. Most commonly, children with AS will be given instruction on speech pragmatics (staying on topic, learning the proper give-and-take of a conversation), inference (guessing what something is about based on context), nonliteral language (puns, jokes, idiomatic expressions, metaphors), nonverbal language (body language, facial expression, eye gaze), intonation and inflection (working on the prosody and rhythm of the voice), and comprehension and meaning of language.

- ❏ **Behavioral/Psychological Therapy**
  Behavioral and psychological therapy also covers a broad range of services. The most frequent interventions in this category are teaching social skills (how to make friends, how to interact appropriately with other children and adults) and behavior modifications designed to either unlearn distracting or destructive behaviors (impulsivity, temper tantrums, crying, hitting, and so on) or to learn new strategies (how to react if you're not picked for a special project, how to help a friend, how to ask for help in class, for example). Some of these skills may be taught by a speech and language therapist, rather than a psychologist.

- ❏ **Occupational (OT)/Physical Therapy (PT)**
  Occupational or physical therapy in this context is

designed to help children with fine- and gross-motor skills, such as pencil work, manipulating objects, posture, gait, and hand-eye coordination, as well as balance, if needed. OT or PT work is often left off of IEPs for students with AS. If your child has significant issues in any of these areas, insist that accommodations or instruction be added to her IEP.

❐ **Academic Support**
Apart from the special services your child might need, there may be one or more academic areas where he is weak. Often, this is accepted as "normal," and no services will be provided. If you feel strongly about a deficit, you can try to fight it, and get help for areas where your child is struggling, especially if there is a vast differential between his abilities in one academic area (for example, he gets A's in mathematics) and another area (he gets C's and D's in writing). Also be on the lookout for other learning disorders – your child may have a secondary learning disorder, such as dyslexia, that has not yet been diagnosed.

❐ **In-Class Assistance**
Fairly frequently, a child is so deeply affected by AS that he can barely make it through his day. He cannot get his materials out of his desk on time, he cannot move through a lesson plan without direct intervention, he falls apart at each transition, and he is so overwhelmed by life that he constantly strikes out at other children.

If your child cannot make it through the day without a major meltdown, request an aide to shadow her throughout the school day. If your child's behaviors are so pronounced as to be a true disruption in the class, this should be a no-brainer on the part of the district: The classroom teacher cannot give your child the help she needs, and the rest of the class will suffer because of your child's inability to cope.

Sometimes a district will place an aide in a class to help with one or more children. This is fine as long as your child is given enough support. If he is still overly disruptive and falling apart, insist that he receive a full-time aide. If the district refuses, ask what they recommend given the situation, which clearly is untenable for all parties. Most districts are loath to move a child to a special education class or center, and current federal law makes this an absolute last choice, as all children are to be taught in the "least restrictive environment" (LRE). But if nothing else works, this may be the best choice, at least for the time being. Having your child disrupt the entire class serves no one – not the teacher, not the other children, not the school, and most of all not your child. He is not able to learn if he is in this much turmoil, and a situation like this is probably exacerbating his problems.

How to Write a Goal and an Objective

Goals and objectives are like menu planning and recipes. Goals (the menu: Spaghetti with meatball, crusty rolls, green salad, and ice cream for dessert) must be meaningful and specific. Objectives (the recipes: How you prepare each dish) must address exactly how each goal will be met, including success criteria.

First, let's look at a "mathematical" equation that helps to determine what your child needs:

Normal Range – Present Level of Performance = Need

The normal range is where most children are in a given area, emotionally, behaviorally, physically, or cognitively. The present level of performance (sometimes called the PLOP) is where your child is right now. The difference between the two reflects the specific need your child has. That need (or some increment of a longer-term need that cannot be met in one school year) is the goal.

Let's look at another "mathematical" equation:

$$Need/Measurable\ Steps = Objectives$$

By taking the "need" (the goal) and dividing it into smaller and measurable steps, you can come up with objectives that will work. This is the recipe – how you will achieve the goal and in what increments. To make this clearer, let's look at a case study.

The Case of Jimmy

Jimmy is 8 years old; he was diagnosed with AS when he was 5. He has difficulty sitting still in class and keeping his hands and legs to himself. He rarely maintains eye gaze with parents, teachers, or peers. He gets frustrated easily and cannot complete schoolwork within the given time. As a result, he often has to take work home to finish, on top of his homework, which causes problems at home, according to his mother. He is learning cursive with the class, but has a hard time holding the pencil lightly enough so that he does not break the lead. He labors very hard when doing pencil-and-paper work, and his handwriting is only about 50% legible. He has a very difficult time working with other children; he frequently calls children names and sulks if a peer or a group does not do as he asks. His conversations only last for two exchanges before he turns the conversation to himself or Pokémon. He does not like P.E., and when he is coerced into playing a game, he is unable to follow the rules or follow through on most physical requirements, such as throwing or catching a ball, which causes him to fall apart and cry. Recess and lunchtime are equally stressful: He sits by himself or swings by himself. The children tease him and get angry with him at line-up because he cannot keep himself from touching the other kids or bumping them accidentally.

Appropriate Goals and Objectives

First and foremost, the goal or objective must be appropriate for your child's needs. For example, if you have a program for autism spectrum children in your school district, there may be a desire to place your child on a cookie-cutter IEP that has been used for all other students with AS, NLD, and HFA. This is not following the spirit of the law. Each child's educational plan must be individualized, so to say that all AS children always need services x, y, and z misses the mark entirely.

While it may seem harmless to give your child services that she doesn't really need, remember that every time she is pulled out of the classroom for services means less time that she is mainstreamed – and being in the mainstream should be the goal for every child. If your child needs services, she should get them, by all means. But remember that there is a trade-off for too many services.

A far more common situation is that children with AS don't get all of the services they need. For example, your child may be given physical therapy because the district has a physical therapist, even though what your child really needs is occupational therapy. Your child may be placed with a speech teacher whose emphasis is on articulation when what the child needs is speech pragmatics and social skills instruction. Not only must the goals and objectives be appropriate, the way in which they are carried out must be appropriate as well.

Using the case study above, the following areas of intervention might be appropriate for 8-year-old Jimmy:

- ❐ Social skills training to learn empathy, conversation skills, personal boundaries, nonverbal language.

- ❐ Physical therapy to work on gross-motor skills such as ball work, balance, and coordination.

- ❐ Occupational therapy to work on fine-motor skills such as drawing, printing, and cursive writing, as well as learning calming/arousing strategies to keep his fidgeting from annoying classmates and his teacher.

- ❐ Executive functioning instruction (how he manages time and materials) to help him organize his time better, possibly including an analog clock or timer for his desk and a binder organizer that helps him keep his paperwork straight.

- ❐ Reduction of schoolwork and homework.

- ❐ Classroom aide to help him stay on topic, help him get his work done, and help him in transitioning.

- ❐ Playground modifications of taping a line for Jimmy to stand on when lining up.

- ❐ Classroom modifications of a T-Stool (a one-legged stool) or therapy ball for Jimmy to sit on to help him stay focused in class.

So, one appropriate goal for Jimmy might be:

Jimmy will improve his printing and cursive hand-writing so that it is 100% legible, with less than one error per paragraph, and be able to keep up with the rest of the class in written tests by the end of the school year.

An appropriate set of objectives for Jimmy might be as follows:

- ☐ By Nov. 1, Jimmy will use the "Handwriting Without Tears" methodology and chalkboard and demonstrate the ability to properly form all letters of the alphabet in printing, and letters A through L in cursive.

- ☐ By Jan. 1, Jimmy will use a chalkboard and demonstrate the ability to properly form letters M through Z in cursive, and will be able to print with 100% legibility with pencil and paper, with no more than one formation error per sentence.

- ☐ By Apr. 1, Jimmy will form all printed and cursive letters with 100% legibility with pencil and paper, with no more than one formation error per sentence.

- ☐ By the end of the school year, Jimmy will be able to keep up with the rest of the class when writing answers on tests, and his handwriting will be 100% legible and with no more than one formation error per paragraph.

Three Cardinal Rules for Writing Good Goals and Objectives

❑ They must be SPECIFIC. The goal and its corollary objectives must be very specific about the changes that should occur through intervention: "Will form all printed and cursive letters."

❑ They must be MEASURABLE. Goals and objectives also must be measurable so that you and the administrator will know that the goals have been met: "Will be 100% legible with paper and pencil."

❑ They must be TIME-BOUND. Putting a time constraint on performance is vital. If an intervention does not succeed by the time stated, you have the right to ask for another type of intervention: "By November 1."

More IEP Trials and Tribulations

Many districts commit IEP errors, with or without intention, for reasons of economics or because of time constraints or ignorance of the law. Regardless of the reason, you must be aware of some of the common trip-ups.

School District Failure to Provide Assessment Reports and Tentative IEP Plan to Parents Prior to Meeting

There are few things more nerve-wracking than reading an assessment report about your child right before an IEP meeting while five people watch you, knowing that you have a limited time to get through the report. This, though not illegal as far as I can ascertain, is still a major no-no.

Always request, in writing, that you receive a copy of the tentative IEP and all assessments done for your child at least three days prior to the IEP meeting, which is your legal right. You need time to read through everything and figure out if there are any holes or misleading information. Doing so in front of the school staff, who are tapping their feet wanting to get on with the meeting, is not enough.

Further, the district may hand you a form with virtually no services on it while in the meeting. It takes an incredibly quick-witted person to identify the problem, regain composure, and insist on services not listed – all in a few minutes.

The Required Services Are Not Available

A failing of some IEPs is that districts will tell you that the services that your child needs – even if the district agrees your child needs them – are "not available," or cost too much. However, federal law states that it is illegal to withhold needed services for any reason. If the district does not currently have someone on staff to provide the needed services, it must retain someone or pay for your child to attend a private school that does provide the services, regardless of the financial hardship to the school district.

Failure to Inform Parents of Available Services

Related to this failing is another error – that of omission. Occasionally, a school administrator may know of a certain intervention that might help your child but fail to tell you because it would be difficult or costly to supply. The reason is this – if the district tells you about a program that might help your child, you could turn around and legally insist that the district supply this service.

In tight economic times, it's understandable that districts aren't eagerly offering to spend more money on special services. The downside is that many well-meaning parents who would gladly pay for the services themselves never learn of interventions that could truly help their children.

If you do pay for extra services outside of the district, make sure that this is noted on your child's annual IEP; for example, "Parents will send child to summer social skills camp to improve skills in this area." It's important to have a written record stating what you have done as a parent to supplement the IEP.

Failure to Provide Requested Assessments

Failure to properly assess a child, or telling you that your child does not need assessments that you have requested, is illegal. You have the right to ask that any assessment be performed on your child as long as it relates to his disability. I don't recommend asking for a full battery of tests at every opportunity to ferret out each tiny little issue (that would be a waste of time and energy on everyone's part), but if there are significant issues that are causing your child hardship in school, press for the assessment. If the district says your child doesn't need it, remind them that you will file a formal complaint unless they provide the assessments.

Failure to Appropriately Individualize an IEP

Upon occasion, IEPs are not appropriately individualized, for example, by placing a child in the mainstream setting and giving him services in a pullout class (speech or re-source class) but failing to modify the mainstream learning program or environment to meet his needs in the regular classroom. Your child's entire educational experience should be individualized to meet his needs, if necessary. This may mean changes to his homework load, to his desk and chair, position in the classroom, types of pencils and pens he uses, and so forth.

Blaming the Child or the Parent for Failure of Interventions

Another major IEP evil is finger-pointing, either at your child's behavior or at your behavior as a parent, as impeding the child's progress. Here's a Present Level of Performance excerpt from Will's annual IEP evaluation after he completed kindergarten:

> *"Will continues to be inconsistent in his willingness to follow very direct 'commands' or structure. While usually easy-going and flexible (the last 2 months or so have been particularly successful and happy for Will), he has become very defiant and resistant at times throughout the year."*

Remember, this was a 5-year-old (children that age are a pretty defiant and resistant lot to begin with) with a fairly severe presentation of AS at the time. While it may have been convenient for the speech pathologist to say that Will was consciously misbehaving (his "inconsistent willingness") and that his behavior was inappropriate ("very defiant and resistant"), she did *nothing* to address these issues in the IEP. If there are any issues noted in a PLOP, they must be addressed by the IEP.

The second problem with this PLOP is that it misses entirely the root cause for the child's behavior – his disorder! Most young kids with AS lack the ability to consciously misbehave. What this speech pathologist missed was that Will was *unable* to follow directions consistently (therefore, his inability should have been addressed as a real issue). Further, he was unable to respond properly in certain situations (never named), and therefore acted in a way that seemed to be contrary at times.

Here's an excerpt from a far more well-balanced PLOP from another speech pathologist after third grade:

> *"His egocentric-like behaviors often created distance between him and the other members of a group. He now appears to be more aware of social boundaries, and attempts to choose his words carefully ... He often questions the validity of an activity, but it appears that he is beginning to be able to negotiate the conflict he has between his own desires and what is required of him."*

These are virtually the same behaviors, but now described without blame (and being addressed in his IEP, as the teacher describes how he is improving over time). She framed Will's resistance for what it really was – AS egocentricity, something tangible that can and should be addressed.

A related IEP sin worth mentioning is the language "the student will choose ..., " as in "Jimmy will choose better strategies than name-calling," or "Jimmy will choose to use his time more wisely in class." This insinuates that Jimmy has *consciously been making bad choices* all along, and minimizes the impact that his disorder has on him. This is the same as blaming the child for his deficits. If you see this type of language on your child's IEP, insist that it be reworded to "Jimmy will be able ... " There is a huge difference between ability and choice, and IEPs should accurately reflect your child's ability.

Your Input and Responsibilities as a Parent

You have serious responsibilities for helping your child succeed, both at school and at home. Teachers can only do so much in a busy classroom, and you must recognize that any IEP is a joint effort between school and family.

While it's egregious for a teacher to blame your child for not being able to sit still, it is equally egregious for you to blame your child's teacher for your child's inability to sit still. You're a team – you need to work together to come up with solutions that work. It is not the teacher's job to make all of your child's issues simply vanish.

If your child comes to school every day tired and unkempt, get her to bed earlier and teach her basic hygiene skills. That's your job. If your child is disrupting the class with her GameBoy, make sure she leaves it at home, no matter how much she fusses. Hide the thing if you have to! If your child is allowed to call her siblings names at home, you'd best stop that behavior there, because she will likely never stop this behavior at school if she is allowed to do it at home.

In short, you must do your part to ensure that your child is able to succeed throughout the day. Your child's behaviors at school often are a mirror of her behaviors at home, and every staff person in your school district knows it.

How to Read an IEP (and Prepare for an IEP Meeting)

With a bit of luck (or by formally requesting it from the district), you will have all of the assessments and the tentative IEP before the meeting so that you can go through all the documents and read them carefully. Use this checklist to organize your thoughts and questions.

❑ Note carefully if your child has been qualified, and how he qualified. Will he receive services? Are the goals and objectives clear and sensible? Is anything missing?

❑ If you think there are problems with the IEP or assessment, write down what and why. If you think that there are interventions that should be offered, write those down, too. Formulate better goals and objectives, if need be.

❑ Make sure you look for some of the "major sins" noted in the previous section, and ask that the language be changed if it sounds as though you or your child are being blamed for anything in the present level of performance sections.

❑ If your child has received interventions outside the school during the past year, or will over the summer, make sure those are included.

❑ Be prepared to negotiate what items should be added, changed, or deleted. The administrator of the IEP should make notes as to what these changes are and send you an amended copy.

Know What You Are Signing

Because the IEP is a legal contract between you and the district, it is important to know what your rights are when you sign it. If you have asked for several changes, ask that the IEP forms be retyped so that they include all of your changes before you sign the document. If there are just a few, handwritten changes are fine. If the team tells you that they will agree to all the things you've discussed and make the changes later, I urge you not to sign until the changes are added. Things are easily forgotten, and if something is not included when you sign the document, you may not be able to get it in later.

If you have hit an impasse in the IEP meeting, you can refuse to sign the IEP. Districts dislike this, because it means that the IEP is automatically out of compliance. If they cannot resolve the issues directly with you, they have to go to due process. They may try to pressure you to sign the document, but if the IEP truly is in bad shape or totally off the mark, going to due process may be the only way to fix the problem.

If you agree on nearly everything, but didn't get one or two smaller points across, my recommendation is to sign the IEP and consider getting these extra services outside of the district. You are unlikely to get everything you want for your child, so focus on what he needs most right now.

Your Addendum

You have the right to ask that a parent's statement be attached to your child's IEP. This is especially important if you and the district disagree about key elements of the contents. For example, if the district is blaming your child for misbehaving rather than framing the behavior as part of her disability, and they refuse to change the language in the IEP to your satisfaction, write up a paper stating your beliefs and ask that it be attached to the IEP. If the team administrator refuses to do so, contact the district. If you still meet with refusal, you can file a formal complaint. See Letter to File a Complaint in the Resources & References section for more information.

The IEP Team and the Administrator

All IEP teams look different, and have different members associated with them. Also, your child's IEP team will likely change over time – this is to be expected. Here is a rough outline of how most IEP teams are composed.

Roles of the IEP Team Members

Every IEP must have an administrator who is responsible for oversight of the entire IEP. Often this is the special education teacher. His or her job will be to keep in touch with the various IEP team members to see how your child is doing and report back, via the IEP form, to you at regular intervals (three or four times a year).

Other likely members of the IEP team include your child's classroom teachers and perhaps the principal. Because most of your child's day will be in a general education class if mainstreamed, the teachers' input is vital to the IEP process: What are the child's relative strengths, weaknesses, areas of particular concern, and so forth?

The IEP team should also include all the specialists who work with your child, such as the school psychologist, occupational therapist, P.E. instructor or physical therapist, and so forth.

The final members of the IEP team, and most important in my mind, are the child's parents. As parents of a child with special needs, the law mandates that you be part of the IEP process and team. The rest of the team cannot take action against your will, unless a court has decided through due process that they can.

The First IEP Meeting

The first IEP meeting can be a harrowing experience. Every time I go into a meeting I have the sense that I've been called into the principal's office – old memories are hard to suppress! Read through the following section, do your homework, take a deep breath, and don't be intimidated.

Who Will Be There

The IEP is supposed to be executed as a team. This means that many people participate on an IEP team and are expected to contribute to it.

You are part of that team, and nothing can happen to an IEP without your agreement. This is important to remember. You are also allowed to bring anyone (within reason) to an IEP meeting, so long as you have notified the district in writing, usually within three days before the meeting. The district must also notify you of who will be attending on their behalf.

Generally, the following people will be at the first IEP meeting:

- ❏ You, the parent(s)

- ❏ The director of special education for the school district

- ❏ The principal of your child's school

- ❏ Your child's teacher

- ❏ The school's (or district's) speech-language therapist

- ❏ The school's (or district's) psychologist/resource teacher

Additionally, the district may bring in other people, such as teachers who have had more experience working with AS children, or outside assessors.

You may bring any of the following with if you notify the district in writing in advance:

- ❐ A friend for support (especially useful if you are a single parent and feel overwhelmed)

- ❐ An educational advocate

- ❐ A specialist in AS, such as a speech therapist, psychologist, occupational therapist

- ❐ An advocate for children with special needs

While you can bring just about anyone to the meeting, know that if you bring a whole cadre of people, the district is likely to take a negative view of your approach. But if you think that bringing one person, maybe two, can help you make the case more effectively, by all means do it. These people will not be considered part of the team, but you are free to call on them to support the team as needed.

What You Need

In the best of situations, you don't need anything to walk into an IEP meeting, except for your wits and common sense. However, in most cases, it is best to plan ahead and have your case well documented.

What this means is to have all of your paperwork: the binder you've started with all of the legal letters and responses, all of the outside assessment reports you've received from the district, as well as any assessment reports and diagnoses you have obtained yourself for your child. If any of the assessments your child has received so far include suggestions for intervention, be prepared to bring those up in the meeting.

I also suggest that you do some research on what types of interventions are most commonly used for your child's deficits. Also refer to the section IEP Goals and Objectives to get an idea of how these are written up. Write up the types of interventions that you think would benefit your child, and make copies for each person at the meeting. The IEP meeting should be interactive. Although the district should provide experts on what types of interventions will be best for your child, you also have input. And because you know your child better than anyone, your input is very valuable.

What You Should Be Prepared For

In the best of circumstances, IEP meetings are open exchanges of ideas and suggestions for the benefit of the child, and that is often how they work. But sometimes what the child needs seems to get lost, as administrators whine (yes, whine) about lack of funds and resources, parents get hostile and nasty, and teachers mumble, "Well, Johnny seems to be doing well; he just needs to try harder; that's all!"

Hope for the best, prepare for the worst. Keep your cool. Make your assertions, over and over again, if need be. Come up with innovative approaches if you can, and prepare to negotiate on certain items (you will probably never get everything you want for your child, and it's not reasonable to expect that you would).

Don't negotiate to the point that your child loses important interventions. If the district tries to talk you out of speech and language intervention, for example, and you know that your child needs help in this area, you can refuse to sign the IEP and ask for due process. This rarely happens, but know that you do have the right (if not the responsibility) to stick up for what your child needs.

The Whole-Child Approach

Because we place such a huge emphasis on academics in our country, a key aspect of an IEP that is often missed is that the whole child needs to be considered. This means that even though your child does well in class and at home, if he is falling apart every time he goes outside to play, the IEP must consider this as a deficit as it prevents him from being successful throughout the school day.

Further, if your child gets through the day in a substandard way (but still within the parameters of "normalcy") but then throws wild tantrums the minute he gets home from school, he is also likely to qualify for services. This last example is controversial, in that the child "gets through the day" all right and his major breakdowns occur at home. However, many children, and children with AS in particular, save up their release of stress and anxiety for a place and time when they know they are safe – at home. It is not a huge stretch, then, to state that your child is under such pressure at school just to get by that he is falling apart at home. Ergo, he should (you insist) qualify for additional help in school to alleviate the stress.

Here is a breakdown of school day activities to think about as potentially strong or weak areas for your child as you prepare for your child's initial (or subsequent) IEP meeting:

Subject Area		Any Concerns?
Academics	Spelling	
	Reading ability	
	Reading for comprehension	
	Vocabulary	
	Writing mechanics	
	Expressive writing	
	Mathematics	
	Science	
	Social studies	
In-class behavior	Respect for teacher	
	Listening well	
	Following instructions	
	Impulse control	
	Peer relationships	
	Group relationships	
	Organization	
	Use of time	
	Homework and class work being turned in on time	
	Asking for help when needed	

Subject Area		Any Concerns?
Playground behavior	Respect for/understanding of rules	
	Joining in games	
	Playing by self	
	Peer/group relationships	
Transition behavior	Understands/follows rules	
	Impulse control	
	Peer/group relationships	
P.E.	Understanding/following rules	
	Motor skill functioning	
	Impulse control	
	Peer/group relationships	
Art	Motor skill functioning	
	Following instructions	
Music	Motor skill functioning	
	Following instructions	
At-home behavior	Understanding/completing homework	
	Staying on task	
	Bringing materials home	
	Asking for help when needed	

You are not looking for perfection in every area. Rather, you are looking for areas of notable weakness throughout the school day. If your child is only so-so at sports, for example, this would not qualify him for an occupational therapist. If, however, he is consistently unable to catch a ball by second grade, it probably would qualify him.

Also, in academics, many kids with AS excel in some areas (most notably math and science) and have a rough time in others (expressive writing, for example). Many have an ability gap between one subject and another, and this is considered "normal" unless there is a significant enough gap to warrant further assessment. For example, if your child consistently scores in the high 90th percentile in math, but is scoring in the 50s or 60s in reading comprehension, you may have an issue that needs attention. A gap of more than 25-30 percentage points in different areas may be a cause for concern as it shows a potential cognitive deficit due to disability.

What to Do Next

If you've got your binder, some writing paper and a pen, your assessments, your observations about weak areas, and your ideas for possible interventions, goals, and objectives, you're ready to go. Take a deep breath, and walk through the door. Good luck!

IEP Meetings – Interim, Annual, Triennial

IEP meetings can happen any time any member of the IEP team has any concerns large enough to warrant a meeting and reopening the IEP for modification. However, IEP meetings usually occur on a regular schedule, once every year.

The Right Time of Year

Most districts hold annual and triennial IEP meetings in the late spring, so that the IEP team can review the progress made through an entire school year, and plan what goals and objectives should be on the IEP for the following year.

This is to the benefit of the child. It means that there will be a signed IEP in place the minute he sets foot in the school the following year, and interventions and services can begin immediately. If the IEP meeting is pushed off until just before the school year, it may be difficult, if not impossible, to get the IEP done before the start of the school year.

Make sure you have adequate leeway if you believe there might be any difficulty working out the details. Once summer comes, the school staff (and you as well) are likely to be headed for summer vacations, and federal law or not, it is difficult to organize an IEP team meeting over the summer or resolve disputes. Ensure that your annual meeting is no later than mid-May if your school lets out in mid-June.

A Word of Warning

In one instance, the child's IEP meeting was held the second-to-last day of school. The meeting ended in gridlock. The parents asked for additional assessment so that they could prove that their child needed social services interventions. The bureaucratic wheels turned slowly, and the assessment didn't happen until nearly the end of the summer. The report came in after the school year had started, and then there was another delay in setting up the next IEP meeting. Another round of battling (the assessment didn't prove or disprove much of anything), and the parents finally went to due process right before the winter break. The case was settled in the family's favor, and the child was given services, but not until late February. This child had lost almost two-thirds of a school year's worth of intervention. Get those assessments done early, and make sure your IEP meeting is held no later than May to give you adequate time to move on any outstanding issues.

Interim IEP Meetings

You have the legal right to request an interim IEP meeting at any time. However, I recommend that you try not to exercise this right unless you really have to, as it can cause contention between you and the district. (See Who to Turn to If the IEP Isn't Working below.)

If you do have major issues and an IEP meeting is the only way they can be reasonably addressed, send a request for an interim IEP in writing to the IEP administrator, with a copy to the director of special needs services. The administrator should contact you and set up an interim meeting without delay. If you do not hear anything after a week or so, contact the director. If you still do not hear back, file a formal complaint.

Annual IEP Meetings

Annual IEP meetings are just that – the annual meeting, preferably late in the school year, where the team members get together to discuss your child's progress and begin to make plans for the following year.

If there have been any major issues during the year, you can request assessment prior to the meeting so that any new or emerging issues can be dealt with immediately. Prepare for each IEP meeting the way you would for your initial IEP meeting: Ask for the tentative IEP in advance, as well as any additional information from your child's regular teachers, aides, or other service providers. If any assessments have been done, make sure you have read them thoroughly.

The annual meeting should be the big event of the year with regard to your child's IEP. Reopening an IEP each time you have a small concern or new idea for an intervention will be viewed dimly by the district. The more you can cover in these meetings the happier the team will be, as will your child.

Pay particular attention to the goals and objectives from the past year. Were they met? Was the child successful in meeting the goals? If not, do not let the district simply add them to the next year, and try the same intervention again. It didn't work this year, why should it work next year? Insist that they change strategies.

Triennial IEP Meetings

Every three years the district must reassess your child to see if she still qualifies for an IEP according to federal law. Long before the actual meeting, you should receive an assessment notice from the district, informing you that they will be performing certain assessments on your child to ascertain ongoing eligibility. Don't panic; your child is not being singled out, this is the way the process is supposed to work.

Take a hard look at the assessment and observation tools that the district is planning to use. Look at the Assessments section and see if the tools the district is planning on using will help or hinder your case. Remember, you have the right to request any assessment at any time, but now is the best time to request additional assessment. Despite the cost, my recommendation is to ask for the "whole enchilada" every three years. This gives a fresh baseline from which to start. Children's abilities change over time in all areas. Just because your child was in the normal ranges for her age three years ago does not mean she is still within those ranges now.

Because of its comprehensive approach, and the fact that it is designed for children with this type of disability, I recommend asking that the district use NEPSY (see page 107) once every three years to assess your child. Additional tests may be warranted as well, depending on your child's types and levels of disabilities.

The triennial is also the ideal time to rethink long-term goals. Are they still applicable? Has your child made appropriate progress? This is the time to think ahead longer term, though of course you can do so at any point in the process.

Discontinuing an IEP

Triennials are nerve-wracking because there is a possibility that the district will try to discontinue the IEP during this process. This is why it is particularly important that they do a full assessment on your child and that you have access to the tentative IEP and all the assessment reports prior to the meeting. If you suspect the district is trying to discontinue your child and you feel that to do so would be improper, you'll need some time to think through your strategies.

First off, IEPs should be discontinued for some children. A child who needs an IEP in first grade does not necessarily need one for the rest of his academic career. However, with AS, it's a slightly different story. Children do not "grow out" of AS – it's a lifetime disorder. Just because a child has mastered his world at one stage does not mean that he won't have trouble at the next stage, either cognitively, behaviorally, or socially. These kids don't get "cured."

For this reason, I recommend insisting that either an IEP or a 504 Plan continue throughout the child's school years, even if no services are being offered. You can't foresee what is going to happen from year to year with these kids as they transition from lower elementary to upper elementary and from elementary to junior high or middle school and then to high school.

It's not to say that once an IEP is closed you can never open another one, but it is very difficult to open an IEP for a child past elementary school, and once you do manage to reopen one, a great deal of time may have been lost. If you feel that your child no longer needs an IEP, and the district agrees with you, you may decide to close the IEP. You know your child best, and should make the decisions based on your knowledge.

Signs of IEP Trouble

Besides the "gotchas" listed in the previous sections, there are a few other warning signs to watch for. One is that the team (or some representative of the school district) is planning to discontinue your child's IEP at the next triennial without your prior approval to do so. This has happened to us at both of our triennials, and I'm guessing it will happen at our next.

In speaking to other parents, I learned that there seems to be a pattern to how this is done. It goes something like this: Appropriate services are offered in the first year. Goals are met, and services are somewhat reduced in the second year, because your child has mastered some of his deficient areas. In the third year, services are reduced further, and very few if any interventions are included on the IEP. Additionally, parents report resistance to adding new goals and objectives to the IEP (the school district may insist that your child is "within normal ranges" in that particular area, and doesn't need any further intervention).

In my child's IEP history, at grade 3 (his first triennial), I was sent an IEP for review with no social skills or pragmatic language intervention in it. I was livid – Will was still struggling socially and had no friends. Second grade had been horrible for him, and he was still being teased on a regular basis. I was astounded when his speech pathologist claimed he had no more need for intervention. I fought the district by insisting on outside assessment by a local expert on AS and by providing a second report from Will's original diagnostician, at my own expense. The district acquiesced (Will got one measly social skills goal), and the next year, we had a new and very effective speech pathologist who helped Will immensely, going far beyond what the IEP from the previous year had outlined.

Will's next triennial process was equally mangled. Halfway through the school year, his new speech pathologist (his third in six years) told Will "there's nothing wrong with you; you don't need to come to speech any more!" I had a suspicion of what was coming. Sure enough! When the assessment plan came home for reevaluating Will's needs, the tests presented completed the picture. He was only going to be given sub-tests of CASL (see page 101) and TOPS (see page 103), both of which he would ace. And he did, of course.

The IEP was handled so badly that the district really couldn't close his IEP, even if they had been of a mind to do so. Will's teachers and the principal of the school all felt he needed to continue on the IEP, as did the school psychologist. We prevailed in keeping the IEP open.

Whom to Turn to If the IEP Isn't Working

Sometimes an IEP goes awry midway through the year, and you may need to bring this to the attention of the team. As described below, there is a definite chain of command that should be followed when approaching the team with an issue.

1) After confirming that there is a problem, perhaps with your child's classroom teachers or with the playground supervisor, contact the IEP administrator, outline your concerns and your child's issues, and request a reply. Often, small problems (and even big ones) can be handled directly by the administrator, if the person is well connected in the school district, is knowledgeable, and is willing to work with you. You can contact the administrator by email, regular mail, or phone, but I recommend email or regular mail so there is a paper trail. (Keep copies.)

2) If the administrator does not get back to you within a reasonable length of time, contact him again. If

you don't receive a reply a second time, contact the principal and the director of special needs services simultaneously, stating that you have tried on two occasions to contact the IEP administrator but have received no reply. Outline the issues and your concerns. The director will likely either contact the administrator and make sure you are contacted immediately, or the director may contact you. Take notes of all telephone calls and add them to your personal file.

3) At this point, your goal is to get the IEP back on track. Save any smaller issues for the end of the year when you have your annual IEP meeting. However, if the district does not respond to your concerns, or is delaying unnecessarily, you have the right to request an interim IEP meeting. (You can request an interim meeting at any time, but it is easier, more efficient, and less contentious to try to work out issues without an IEP meeting, when possible.) The district must set up a meeting, and invite all of the standard IEP team members to attend. At this meeting, you can present your case.

4) If at this meeting, or at any other IEP meetings, you are unsatisfied with the results, you can request that due process be put into action. More on this is found under Due Process at the end of this chapter. I recommend retaining an educational advocate to help you through this situation.

Filing a Complaint

If and when an IEP is out of compliance, or when an administrator is out of compliance, you have the legal right to file a formal complaint. Any time a district has violated

IDEA or any state special education laws applicable where you live, the first response is to file a complaint (you can simultaneously file a complaint and request due process). Note that filing a complaint is used when the district has failed to uphold the law; due process is used when you and the district are disputing what services (if any) your child should be receiving under the law.

Reasons to File a Complaint

Some typical reasons why you might file a complaint include the district's ...

- ☐ Failure to contact you within the legal time limit regarding a request to assess for an IEP

- ☐ Failure to provide assessments that you have formally requested

- ☐ Failure to allow you access to your child's files

- ☐ Failure to implement one or more aspects of a signed IEP

- ☐ Failure to give you notice prior to assessments or observations

- ☐ Failure to discuss all aspects of an IEP

- ☐ Failure to notify you prior to changing an IEP or an intervention program

Filing a complaint is a contentious act, and I don't recommend doing it unless something truly is compromising your child's ability to succeed.

For example, one of our speech pathologists read Will's tentative IEP to him, including direct comments from his teachers and his test scores, before I had a chance to review it. This was bad enough, but she read it to him in front of another child, causing them both discomfort. This is clearly a violation of confidentiality, and definitely falls within complaint material. However, my primary concern was with ensuring that it never happened again – there was no other remedy that could be made. For that reason, I went directly to the school district with my complaint. But, I made sure they were aware that I could file a formal complaint if I had wanted to, and indeed could have sued them in civil court as well.

Whom to Notify with a Complaint

Generally, complaints should be sent to the state educational agency. This contact information should be listed in the parent's notice of rights you received when you first requested an IEP assessment. It's best to call first and ask the department to whom you should address and send the information, unless you know specifically who the contact is.

If you live in an area with a local agency (such as at the county level), you may want to copy that agency on your complaint, as they may be the organization that carries out the investigation.

What the Letter Should State

The letter should state your identifying information, including your phone number, and should outline the complaint, including dates, names of people you have spoken with, and so on. If you know what area of IDEA has been violated, you may quote the specific code. Keep it simple and nonjudgmental. Also include a statement of what you feel a reasonable remedy would be, including any reimbursements for costs incurred because of the violation. For example, if you had to send your child to private occupational therapy because the district failed to provide OT service, even though the IEP says they will, include the costs of the therapist, as well as any transportation costs incurred. Keep it simple and straightforward. Sign it, and keep a copy for your records.

What Happens Next

Federal law mandates that the state send you a decision within 60 days. Most likely, the agency will contact you and ask you more questions about the violation, and then will contact the district. Once they have the information, they will notify both parties of their decision.

If the agency judges in your favor, the district will be notified of what actions it must take to rectify the situation, and how long it has to do it. If the district doesn't comply, you can either file another complaint or ask for due process.

Due Process

I'm hoping that you will never have to use the information in this section. Due process is used when you and the district cannot agree on how to proceed on an IEP. Requesting due process means that the IEP process has broken down, and you need to rely on the law to rectify the situation.

Before you turn to due process, you should have tried everything reasonable to work with the district to resolve the case. Mediators and hearing officers look very unkindly on parents (and district administrators) who come to them without having tried to negotiate the issues first. If you cannot resolve your issues with the district, send them a letter indicating that your next course of action will be to request due process – then wait a week before you do so. Miraculously, some districts will find it in their hearts (if not their pocketbooks) to resolve the case directly with the parent.

While this section gives you an overview, I recommend that you study the issues, hire an educational advocate, and hire an attorney to help you. If you've reached this stage, you'll want to proceed with as much intelligence and support as you can muster.

Requesting Due Process

After the lines of communication have broken down and you have reached an impasse with the district, the first step is to formally request due process. This is done by writing a letter (keep a copy) to the state or federal agency handling due process. State that you are requesting due process, beginning with mediation. Call your district administration office for information on where to send requests for due process. They must give you this information, but if they fail to, see the Resources & References section for contact information. State in the letter why you are requesting due process; for example, that despite assessments and observations supporting your claim that your child needs intervention, the district will not comply (or whatever your particular case is).

State what you feel would be appropriate services and why. Indicate that you are aware that the district has 45 days to respond to your request (this may be a shorter period in some states, but the federal law states 45, so stick with that unless you know otherwise).

Sign the letter, and wait for a reply. If you don't hear from the district within the prescribed time period, file a complaint as noted above and let the state agency take care of it. Make sure to keep a record of all your expenses so that you can ask to be reimbursed.

Note that you don't have to start with mediation; you can ask for a fair trial instead. However, mediation is generally less expensive and less time consuming, and it is definitely less contentious. For those reasons, it is generally the course you should take first.

Mediation

After you have sent a letter requesting mediation, you will receive a reply stating the date of the mediation and where it will be held. The mediation itself is carried out by a neutral, third-party mediator selected by the state, who is very well versed in the laws surrounding IDEA and special education in general.

You and the district will both be asked to present your case to the mediator. This presentation should include a brief description of your child (his age, current school and grade level, presenting symptoms, and general areas of deficit); what you and the district are in dispute over; what services you are asking for and why; and a description of your corroborating evidence – assessments, observations, statements from teachers, friends, special needs advocates who have seen your child, and so on. The district will do the same.

After you and the district have made your opening statements, the mediator will meet with both of you privately and discuss the relative strengths and weaknesses of your case. When you are meeting with the mediator, you can speak freely – nothing you say in private to the mediator can be relayed back to the district without your approval. While mediation is not used for levying complaints about violations of IDEA, if you have filed a complaint against the district for one or more violations, by all means bring it up to the mediator. These back-and-forth sessions will continue until an agreement between the two sides has been reached – or until it is clear that no resolution is forthcoming.

You will be expected to negotiate on some items, and so will the district. While you shouldn't give up more than your child can afford, it is often best to accept a compromise to get something done now, rather than prolong the time before your child gets any services.

If you wish, you can bring in outside people to testify at mediation, but generally this strategy is reserved for fair trial (see below), especially if you believe that you may not win mediation. The strategy here is to hold a few cards close to your chest that you can use later in fair trial if necessary. If you show the district all of your cards in mediation, they will have time to work to defend themselves against them later in fair trial.

With a bit of luck, you and the district will reach an agreement, either in whole or in part. If this happens, the mediator fills out a mediation form stating the agreements that were reached and file it with the state. You and the district will also receive a copy. If you do not reach a full agreement, you can agree to try to continue mediation on another day for any remaining items, you can drop any items that were not agreed on, or you can ask to go to fair trial.

If you do not reach an agreement, the mediator will fill out paperwork to that effect. You have the option of dropping the case or going to fair trial.

Fair Trial

Fair trial (sometimes called a fair hearing) ratchets the tension, and the costs, up quite a bit. The process is a lot like a real court trial, but it will not take place in a courtroom, and the "presiding judge" will be an appointed hearing officer. If you have skipped mediation, request a fair trial by sending a letter to the state or federal agency responsible, just as you would for mediation. You will be notified by mail where and when the hearing will be held.

All of your evidence must be submitted in the form of written documents, and all of your witnesses must be sworn in, or you must provide signed and notarized witness affidavits. The office will open the case, explain the process, and both you and the district will give your opening statements.

You (or your attorney) will question all the witnesses you have brought, and the district will be able to cross-examine them. Then the district does the same. Both sides can call back witnesses, and then you can give a closing statement. You will be asked to submit a written brief describing the facts in the case and the laws that pertain to these issues. The hearing officer will render a decision in 45 days. If the verdict is not in your favor, you can appeal the decision.

If this sounds intimidating, that's because it is! While not a real courtroom trial, it's close, and unless you are very well versed on IDEA, have a stout constitution, and think quickly on your feet, you may want an attorney to represent you. At the very least, you will want to spend a great deal of time preparing your case, gathering witnesses, thinking about questions to ask your own and the district's witnesses, and so on. Fair trials are a great deal of work, take a lot of time, and if you use an attorney, may cost you a great deal of money.

To Use an Attorney or Not

Not every family will need to hire an attorney for mediation or a fair hearing. Some cases are so straightforward, and the evidence so overwhelming, that it is not necessary, especially if you are used to speaking in public and can remain unflappable under pressure.

However, for the rest of us mere mortals, an attorney may be the ticket. If you select an attorney who has ample experience in these types of cases, you can leave the majority of the details to him or her. It is, of course, completely up to you to decide if this path is the right one for you to take.

Know that attorney's fees are generally reimbursable to you by the school district if you prevail, with some restrictions and exceptions. Speak to your attorney about reimbursement from the district.

Looking for a New School

If you've run the gamut with the IEP process, and you still believe that your child is not successful in his school environment, you may wish to change schools. This is not a defeatist attitude – it is often wise and practical choice.

Some districts don't understand students with AS, they don't believe the disorder is serious enough to warrant intervention, or they don't know what interventions will work and how to provide them. While it's true that your child is protected under the law and should be granted fair and equal treatment under IDEA, the truth is that she may not be given what she needs.

There are good reasons to change schools. You may have had such a contentious time with your district that the relationship is permanently fouled, and even if they give your child services, they may do so begrudgingly, and be on the lookout for any reason to discontinue services when they can. This is unhealthy for all parties.

Your child may be so in need of help that he has been a major disruption to the class and school in general. While not his fault, he now is marked in a very real way among his peers, and it may take years to undo the damage to his reputation. Starting fresh in a new school may make a huge difference in how he is perceived, especially if he has out-grown some of his more disruptive behaviors.

School districts generally look unkindly on parents who move their children from school to school within a district because a child (or the parents) have burned bridges with the children, families, teachers, and staff. I've seen this happen with children who have defiant or disruptive behaviors; the teachers, in particular, resent being forced to cope with someone else's rejects. In short, if you haven't been successful in a given school, the problem probably exists at the district level, so changing schools within that district may do little, if any, good.

Therefore, you have three options.

1) The first is to find a good private school in your area that offers the services and environment your child needs. You may try to get your school district to pay for it under law, but you may need to pay for it yourself. If you can, do so.

2) The next option is to scout out school districts in your area (only feasible if you live in a large metropolitan area) that are more accepting of children with AS. You can find these districts by joining local advocacy groups and speaking to other parents, or by talking to officials at the local or state agency that handles special education oversight and then request an inter-district transfer.

3) If you cannot get an inter-district transfer, your last option is to move into the preferred district. While this may seem like a radical step, it may be the right one for your child and your family. Every child deserves to succeed, and every parent owes it to his or her children to give them the best they can afford.

Cheap Tricks for the IEP Plan

As in the previous chapter, the primary cheap trick strategy is to keep thorough and complete records of everything that transpires with regard to an IEP. In 10 years you can throw everything out, but for now, save it all!

✋ Make Alliances

One of the best ways to ensure smooth sailing through the IEP process is to have built alliances before the process even begins, and certainly as it progresses. Work with your child's teacher – if possible, become his or her best parent in the classroom! By demonstrating your willingness to be part of the school community, and your willingness to be open to the teacher's suggestions on what will work for your child, you are demonstrating that you are willing to be part of the solution, and not a nag demanding that the teacher fix your child for you.

Having a teacher, a school psychologist, or an administrator on your side as the IEP plan progresses will mean that they will help advocate for your child. If at all possible, you do not want to be the lone voice in an IEP meeting stating that your child needs services. Build the relationships in advance so that you have a virtual harmonious choir, all singing from the same page!

✋ **Keep Your Cool**

I won't lie to you and tell you that every IEP goes smoothly and without hitch. The truth of the matter is that most IEP meetings are a bit nerve-wracking, and a few are out-and-out hostile. IEP meetings are a bit like speed-dating – you have a very limited amount of time to make a good impression. The administrators who attend them see dozens of parents all looking for services for their children. These professionals work very hard, their time is short, and most important, they only see a fraction of your child's history, as presented to them in psychological reports, test results, and teacher's progress reports. If you walk into a meeting on the verge of hysterics or with clenched fists ready to do battle, you will immediately put the IEP team on the defensive. It's okay to be concerned, and it's okay to be fervent in what you say and do, but make sure that these professionals leave the meeting with only the clear knowledge that you are a parent who cares about the welfare of your child and are willing to work with them to make sure he succeeds.

Chapter 6

Life in the Classroom

I have very fond memories of elementary school. All children should have such memories as they grow and mature. Unfortunately, for kids with a disability such as AS, school can be torture. They may not be able to keep up with the other students, whether physically, cognitively, or emotionally. Social interactions may completely baffle them, made doubly difficult because they so badly want to make friends. Children learn so much, or should learn so much, at this magical age, but children with AS often need help to fit in.

The Heart of Your Child's School Day

The classroom is the heart of your child's school day, and most of the focus of his IEP will be targeted at how he performs here. It is where his primary learning occurs, both academically and socially.

Chapter 6

Meeting with the Teachers

Federal law states that all teachers must be made aware of any students with special needs in their classrooms and must have read their IEP or 504 Plan prior to the start of the academic year. My own experience shows that teachers may not have time to read through each form before class starts, relying instead on notes from outgoing teachers or from speech teachers or the principal. This is not necessarily bad, but because there are likely specific things that need to occur in the classroom, you should meet with the teacher to discuss your child's situation at the beginning of the year.

Personally, I like to wait about a week before meeting the teacher, though this may not be prudent in all situations. Let the teacher and the kids settle in a bit so the teacher doesn't feel like you're pouncing on her. Set up a time to discuss your child's needs and circumstances. Fifteen minutes or half an hour should do. Bring a copy of the IEP form with you in case the teacher hasn't had a chance to read it. Discuss what you think are the important things for your child to work on, and explain what interventions are in place and how they will (or should) work in the classroom. Finish the conversation by asking the teacher how she likes to communicate with parents. Some prefer email, others phone calls, others impromptu visits, yet others more formal meetings. Try to be flexible and accommodate the teacher's style. This teacher plays an important role in your child's life, and respecting her wishes helps to create a good relationship.

Some teachers are resistant to the whole notion of having children with special needs along with IEPs and 504s in their rooms. You will recognize these teachers immediately, as they tend to minimize your child's issues. One of my son's teachers refused to read his IEP or to talk to his previous teacher. Her theory was that it would taint her view of him, and she would not be able to see his strengths. She was difficult to work with, and did not want to understand AS or what it was all about. She insisted repeatedly that all of Will's problems would vanish if we simply had him play team sports – there was nothing wrong with him that a little competition and fresh air wouldn't cure!

It was a dreadful year for us, but Will survived. He'd had a great teacher the year before, and had a great teacher the year after, so he didn't lose much ground. If you have a resistant teacher like this, speak to the principal about changing classrooms, but know that most schools frown on this practice. Voice your concern to the powers that be, and hang in there if nothing changes. At the annual IEP meeting, suggest that your child would do much better with a teacher who was more knowledgeable and empathic. Most principals won't willingly make the same mistake twice. If he or she does, go to the superintendent and voice your concerns there.

Understanding the Curriculum

All parents should understand what their children will be learning. This knowledge opens up opportunities for supporting and reinforcing at home, whether it's an extra trip to the planetarium because the class is studying astronomy, mad baking experiments because the kids are learning about chemical reactions, or simply help with homework.

For parents of a child with AS, understanding the curriculum also helps in identifying potential pitfalls. If you know that your child has a hard time with creative writing and you learn that there is a strong focus on this type of writing in a given grade, you will at least be prepared that your child might need some extra help. Similarly, if the kids are going on several field trips and your child is frightened of being away from home, try to see if you can go with your child as a chaperone. Plan ahead.

You should also have a good idea of what the "normal" range of performance is for a particular assignment or subject. This way, if your child falls behind in a subject, you can take action. This means that you will need to communicate with your child's teachers, because the typical grades may not give you an accurate picture of your child's strengths and weaknesses. Maybe all the kids got a D or worse on a given math test, and there's nothing to worry about. But if your child is falling behind, you need to meet with his teachers and plan some intervention to help him.

A final word on curriculum. Often students with AS excel in some areas and have great difficulties in others. Typically, these kids do very well in mathematics and science, but have trouble with writing (both the mechanics and expressive language), P.E., and sometimes reading comprehension, particularly in fiction. Thus, it is entirely possible that your child may be in advanced math, for example, but in remedial spelling. These children are sometimes called Gifted Children with Disabilities, to denote that they are gifted in one area, but have deficits in others. If your school has rules that children cannot be placed in advanced classes if they have low grades in other subjects, challenge that rule as part of your child's IEP process. Make sure your child is allowed to grow and excel in the things he is good at, regardless of his weaknesses.

Setting Expectations

At the beginning of every school year, sit down with your child and your child's teacher individually to set expectations for what your child should be able to accomplish by the end of the year. For most parents, this is pretty simple – such as, we expect you to maintain a "B" average in all of your classes, or such similar high-level expectation.

Your child may need to be given more detailed information and in smaller chunks. For example, although we do have a "B-average rule" in our home, I work with my son on every project or subject unit and discuss what I think he should be able to accomplish, given his abilities. We don't make a big deal out of it, but if, for example, spelling has been a problem, we work a little harder on it, and talk about what we need to do to get an "A" on his tests. Or, if he has a book project due on a book that he had a hard time reading and understanding and we're both just glad to get it done, we may talk about how we can satisfy the requirements.

If your child is having trouble with a subject or a particular assignment, make sure to communicate with his teachers, especially if you've told your child that doing the bare minimum on a given project is okay with you. While I don't recommend letting your kid off the hook on a regular basis, it is sometimes a matter of picking your battles. If this is the case, tell your child's teachers so that everyone knows the score.

If your child is having trouble repeatedly with a subject and his difficulty seems related to his AS (for example, writing assignments), speak to his teacher about the situation and see if a different set of expectations can be set for him. If this is an area of trouble for longer than one school year, make sure that remedial help in the area is part of the next IEP.

Being Open to Suggestions

Your child's teacher is one of the most significant adults in your child's life. It's important that you build a good relationship with this person. Keep in mind that the teacher has been trained in this profession. While you know your child best, your child's teacher usually knows best how to handle her classroom and students.

Having said that, your child's teacher may never have had a student with AS in her room before, and may be bewildered about how to help him. While it's never a good idea to come on as an expert, you can offer some insight into what works for your child. If the teacher is receptive, you could perhaps offer to lend her one or two books on the subject.

Your child's teacher is a professional. Be open to suggestions. Your child's teacher may have ideas that you have never thought of that might work. Don't think that because a teacher has no experience with AS that she can't be an excellent teacher or that she can't come up with creative, innovative ideas that work. Be open to new ideas. No one has the final word on what works every time.

Setting up Communication Channels

Plan on meeting with the teacher a few times throughout the school year and make sure that she is at all IEP meetings. Good communication can often avert a crisis. Make it your job to ensure that you're in contact on a regular basis, but don't bug the teacher so often that she feels like hiding under her desk every time she sees you coming. Remember, there are lots of other kids in her class, too!

Scaffolding Your Child

When a house or a building is painted, the first step is to put up a scaffold – a structure around the building that helps keep everything in place while we work on the building itself. Scaffolding a child is much the same thing – putting processes and interventions in place that help him "stay put" while he works through tough issues.

Debriefing at Regular Intervals

While communicating with your child's teacher is important, it is equally important to communicate with your child about what is happening in school. This may be difficult in the best of situations, as children – especially when they get older – tend to answer questions in monosyllabic grunts. So if you ask, "What did you do in school today," and you get the answer "Stuff," be pleased that your child fits well within the norm. You may have to be more devious to get the information out of him.

Instead, ask questions like, "Tell me three things you learned today," or "Tell me what the best part of your day was, and then the worst part of your day." Asking concrete questions like these helps any child focus on the particulars, and for AS kids, who often either respond with a simple "stuff" or a four-hour description of absolutely everything that happened, this can help get to the heart of his day.

Listen for any recurring themes, such as "Linda hit me again today for the fourth time," "I get really nervous before recess," or "I don't know why we have to read those stupid books, they're so boring." These statements may point to ongoing issues your child is having in class. If necessary, follow up with the teacher.

As part of our daily debriefing in third and fourth grade, I always asked Will whom he played with at recess. This was a good way to keep in touch with how his social skills were doing (not so well, which is why I asked), and it gave me an opportunity to coax him into approaching kids and asking them to play. We eventually made a rule that three days out of the week he had to find other kids to play with. When he was successful at that, we changed the rule to one out of the two daily recesses. Daily debriefings worked in helping him socialize with other kids, on the playground, at the library, or in the computer lab.

Helping in the Classroom

Another excellent way of keeping an eye on your child's progress in school is to volunteer to help out in the classroom. In addition to gaining an overall idea of what is going on, including possibly learning instructional strategies, this gives you a good idea of what his strengths and weaknesses are, letting you see through walls. Gaining a sense of your child's classroom experience can help you view your child holistically.

Helping at school has other side benefits as well. It builds an alliance with the school staff. Further, it can help your child's self-esteem to have you there. Most young children love having their parents come to school. Also, working in the classroom is a good way for you to see the other kids in action, including spotting kids who have a high tolerance or an affinity for your child. These are potential playmates! You will also get to meet some parents, which can help build alliances. Parents you know and trust can help you have eyes at school when you're not there, and give you insight into your child's day.

On the negative side, you may find that your presence in the classroom is disruptive in that your child clings to you or vies for your attention at every opportunity. Some of this is normal kid stuff, but if your child seems to be overly attached and disruptive, you may want to speak to the teacher. I also suggest speaking to your child and letting her know that while you love the attention you get in the classroom, it's making it hard for you to help the other children. You may even need to go so far as to tell your child that any more disruptive behavior will mean that you can't work in the classroom. If she persists, make good on your threat. Quit, and try again in a few months. Most kids grow out of this phase, and will do what they can to keep you coming back.

A Note of Caution

Don't become a hovering mom. Helping in the classroom is great, but not every day, and not in "takeover" mode. Listen for subtle hints from your child's teacher, and remember that your child benefits immensely from interaction with other adults besides you. If it's time to back off a bit, do so graciously!

Setting up Homework Help

Many kids with AS have great difficulty keeping their homework and projects straight, and while they may be able to get the work done, they often leave their assignments or books at school, forget something is due, or lose something that is done – even when it is in their binder, backpack, or desk.

This deficit in executive functioning aggravates parents, teachers, and the child to no end, and is not limited to kids with AS. Work with your child's teacher to come up with strategies that work for all of you. See the Cheap Tricks section later in this chapter for ideas.

Talking About Your Child's Whole Day – Social Learning

While the main focus of school is academic learning, your child is (or should be) learning social skills and life skills at school as well. Sadly, many kids don't learn enough about social skills to foster social independence, so be on the look-out for how your child is doing in this area. Teachers don't generally spend their breaks (the child's recess and lunchtime) monitoring students to see how they are doing, and may not know if your child is socializing well on the playground.

Make sure your child tells you about his relationships with his peers. The only way to make sure you're getting this information is by asking. Ask your child who he plays with. Ask who is sitting next to him in class, and ask how they interact. Do the other children offer to help him? Do they share materials with him? Do they offer age-appropriate encouragement? Or do they tease him, and let others borrow materials but not him? These are important aspects of your child's life, and finding out how he is doing in school should encompass this information.

As with any other kid, your child will likely run into a few kids who seem to have it out for him. This is normal but upsetting to any child, and children with AS tend to be targets for the schoolhouse bully, and may need help in learning how to cope with these kids. Without prodding, try to ferret out enough information to see if the problem will go away or if you need to intervene.

If your child is being picked on by one or more children, speak with his teacher and make sure that he has as little contact as possible with these kids. Telling the teacher in a nonjudgmental way that your child seems to be having trouble with John and Kimmy gives her a head's-up to watch out for these interactions. Kids can be deceptive, and often bullying behavior goes unnoticed by even the most observant teacher.

Remember to encourage your child to engage with other kids. Talk to him about other kids who may like the same sort of thing your child likes, and nudge him to start a conversation. An excellent book on this subject is *Good Friends Are Hard to Find* by Fred Frankel and Barry Wetmore (1996).

Talking About Your Child's Feelings

Along with talking to your child about friends and successes at school go conversations about how he feels about school and life in general. We don't focus on feelings much here in the United States, and especially with boys, we assume that they should just buck up and get through even the toughest of circumstances. Be a man! Toughen up!

My feminist side wants to scream "Hogwash!" but politics aside, we do our kids a large disservice by not asking them to share their feelings with us on occasion. First off, children with AS have a very difficult time gauging their own and others' feelings, and may only be able to distinguish their feelings in rather primitive ways, either sad, bad, glad, or mad.

While this rudimentary distinction is fine for young children, older children (and adults) need to learn the difference between "enraged" and "annoyed" if they are going to be able to respond appropriately to these feelings. If your child only knows "mad" and his reaction to "mad" is to kick somebody or something, he will have a tough time ahead of him. Helping him develop the language to describe feelings is the first step to understanding the nuances of his and others' feelings, and learning how to react.

Second, there is a very high incidence of depression among adolescents with AS. Giving your child time to talk about his feelings and to work through them with you can help avert a serious problem. These children often have deep feelings about their place in life, and take setbacks and difficulties very personally. They also have a tendency to either shut down or act out when stressed or upset. Give your child ample time to share his feelings so you will be better able to help him cope.

Focusing on Your Child's Strengths

To a child whose world seems incredibly difficult and unfair, there may not be much incentive to get up on certain mornings. She has difficulty paying attention in school, the other kids tease her, she lost her homework again, and no one will come over for a playdate. Your AS child is often acutely aware of her deficits, and they weigh heavily on her soul.

At every opportunity, give your child praise, encouragement, affection, and attention for a job well done. I don't mean half-hearted or empty praise. I mean the real deal – your child can tell the difference. If he comes home with a much-sought-after "A" on a spelling test, celebrate. Go out for ice cream or go roller-blading. If your child finally remembers to bring home a permission slip for a field trip, don't remind him that he forgot it four days in a row, tell him that you really appreciate that he remembered to bring it home.

Even his peculiarities are strengths if looked at through the right prism. Does he know the make and model of every refrigerator on the market? Tell him how impressed you are with his knowledge. Does he line up every dinosaur he has before he goes to sleep? Tell him how great it is to take such good care of his toys. Find ways to make him feel good about himself. Your love for him makes a world of difference, especially when that world can often be hard and cold.

Cheap Tricks for the Classroom

✋ Preferential Seating

If your child has a hard time staying focused in class, ask the teacher if he can sit toward the front and center of the room. This makes it easier for the child to stay focused and not wander off looking at all the kids between him and the chalkboard. If your child has difficulty with one or more children, also mention this to the teacher, and ask that your child be placed near tolerant children.

✋ Priming

Children with AS often have a very difficult transitioning from one task to another, and can become agitated easily if they don't know "what comes next." A very simple intervention for this is to work with your child's teacher and have her or a classroom aide explain the upcoming task or event to the child. For everyday occurrences such as an art project, the teacher can simply spend a few minutes with the child one-on-one at the beginning of the project and explain the process.

For more complex or stressful events such as a test, the teacher should spend some time before the test explaining what will happen: I will pass out the tests, and you will have 30 minutes to finish it. Make sure you have your pencil with the soft grip on your desk. If you have questions, please raise your hand, and remember that during a test, you should try to stay in your seat and not go to the water fountain unless you have to.

For unusual events such as field trips, you or the teacher should carefully explain everything that is going to happen, from lining up for the bus, getting on the bus, expected behavior, where the children are going, to what they will do there, when they will eat lunch, and so forth.

This type of priming is useful throughout the day, too. Always try to "prime" your child to 'what happens next.' It will save many a meltdown!

✋ Cues

Kids who have a really hard time staying focused can also benefit from visual, auditory, or sensory cues to help redirect them. Visual cues, in particular, are very useful. These can include a look or pulling an earlobe (useful only if the child looks at the teacher), calling on the child or making a certain noise (clucking a tongue or making a buzzing sound), or laying a hand on her shoulder. All of these prompts work well to redirect, but of course, the child needs to be told what the teacher is trying to do. So signs and other systems must be pre-arranged and agreed on ahead of time.

Other visual cues that are helpful include taping a checklist of steps to be done each day or in each period to your child's desk, or a reminder about when to leave for speech class. Children who have difficulty in managing their time may benefit from a "quiet clock" on their desk. This allows them to set a timer for the 15 minutes the teacher has given them to accomplish a task, so that they can visually keep track of the time left.

One teacher Will had wrote a single word in the corner of the front chalkboard – WRITE – and she'd point to it at the end of each period. It was Will's cue to write down his homework from that period, and it worked like a charm for him.

✋ Homework Help

If your child has trouble with homework, work with his teacher to come up with some strategies that work. Here are some ideas.

Problem	Interventions
Forgets assignments	See if the teacher will write down all homework assignments due that week and send them home on Monday afternoon. Keep this paper at home.
	For grades 3 and up, have your child call another child in her class and get the assignment. Role play the phone call in advance if necessary. (This teaches problem solving; if I don't know what to do, I need to ask someone.)
	Have the child write down all homework due the next day and all long-term assignments due in the next two weeks on binder paper still in her binder (so it doesn't get lost). As many AS children have a difficult time with handwriting, make sure the teacher gives the child extra time to write this information down, or provide help with the writing itself. (Also, consider getting your child help with the physical mechanics of handwriting – how she holds the pencil, how hard she presses, etc. It's well worth the cost and effort.) If your child writes it down, have the teacher sign the paper every day.

Problem	Interventions
Forgets instructions	See if the teacher will send home a brief explanation of assignments. Or try emailing or calling her for details of the assignment.
	For grades 3 and up, have your child call another child in his class and get the assignment. Role play the phone call in advance if necessary.
Forgets books	As part of the homework check-off with the teacher, have the child ensure that he has the appropriate materials in his backpack to do his homework.
	When the child comes home (or when you pick him up), ask him if he has everything he needs to get his work done. If not, and if he is old enough and capable enough, send him back to retrieve the materials.
	For grades 3 and up, have your child call another child who lives nearby to see if he can borrow his or her book for the evening. Have him walk over and get it, or go with him, as appropriate.
Misplaces homework	Have a single place where completed work always goes – in the child's binder or book bag. Make sure that part of your child's homework is to put completed homework away in that location, every single day. Have the child put homework or assignments done in class in the same location. Homework is not completed until it is in this location!
	Have the child clean out his desk at least once a month. If necessary, go in to help him sort through everything, or ask the teacher if she can oversee the job. Fewer things get lost if the desk is cleaned out on a regular basis.

Problem	Interventions
Forgets to turn homework in	Ask the teacher if she can assign a specific time each day, preferably first thing in the morning, when all homework gets turned in.
	Ask the teacher if she can put out a basket for all homework to go into, and work with your child to turn in all homework and assignments first thing in the morning.
Procrastinates on homework	At school, have the teacher keep an eye on your child to make sure she is working on the appropriate task. Many kids with AS are daydreamers and time wasters and will take up enormous amounts of time sharpening pencils if not redirected.
	Have the teacher set a timer and place it on your child's desk to remind him how much time he has to complete a task.
	At home, remove all distractions from the vicinity, and give your child a quiet place to work. As in school, keep an eye on him to make sure he is doing his work and not staring at the walls. Give gentle redirects to keep going.
	Set a timer for 10 or 15-20 minutes. When the timer goes off, let your child take a 5-minute break to burn off some steam. For example, you may want to have him work for 15 minutes, and then allow him to scooter around the block or jump on a trampoline for 5 minutes and then resume the homework.
	Make sure your child has enough energy to do the work. Give him a snack if necessary.
	For larger projects, help your child break down the assignment into smaller chunks to be done on different days to get the project finished in time. Nothing promotes procrastination faster than being overwhelmed and not knowing where to begin.

✋ Engine Changers

I won't go into too much detail on this subject, because the theory and application is so beautifully handled in the book *The Out-of-Sync Child* by Carol Kranowitz (2006), which I heartily recommend for all parents.

In a nutshell, many children, and children with AS in particular, have a hard time keeping their internal "engines" running at the right speed. They are either running too fast or too slow, slumped over in a chair, nearly falling asleep, or fiddling with everything on their desk and driving the teacher wild.

Helping your child adjust her "engine" is very helpful. Kids who have a hard time paying attention, for example, often need a source of external stimulus to keep them on track. This might include physical activity such as swinging, running, jumping, or may be physical stimulation such as sucking on sour candy, chewing crunchy celery, or drinking cold water.

Some kids also benefit from squeeze balls, Wikki Stix (bendable wax sticks), modeling clay, and other acceptable fidgets to play with, quietly of course, as they listen or work in school and at home. (See A Quick-Pick List of Sensory Stimuli in Chapter 9 for more ideas.)

Kids who are jumping out of their skins have already found a way to get the stimulus they need, but often it is distracting, and not appropriate for the classroom. Work with the teacher to find ways your child can get the stimulus he needs to keep on track by being a classroom helper, walking the roll call to the office, and so forth.

✋ Aligning with Tolerant Children

As mentioned elsewhere, one of the greatest gifts you can give your child is the gift of tolerance, both of him and for him. Do your best to find the tolerant, mellow kids in your son's school, church, synagogue, camps, and so forth, and arrange playdates with them. If things work out, and you feel you can trust these children's parents, you may want to share with them that your son has a disorder. By naming his difference, you can help them help their children learn more about the world around them with sensitivity and compassion.

It's also important to remember that success breeds success. Once your child has had one or two successful friendships, others are easier to come by.

✋ Avoiding Intolerant Children

The flip side of pairing up with tolerant children is avoiding intolerant ones. I'm not talking about the run-of-the-mill, average kid who says the occasional nasty remark or gets into a scuffle once in a while. I'm talking about the out-and-out mean kids who seem to thrive on making others' lives miserable. Luckily, there aren't a lot of truly intolerant, bullying kids, but there are some, and they have a way of singling out the socially awkward kids and making their lives miserable. When possible, try to avert interactions with these kids, although that's easier said than done. If things get out of hand, speak to the adult in charge and, nonjudgmentally, ask that he or she try to keep the two kids apart. Also, work with your child to develop strategies for handling bullies. This is a skill he will likely need time and time again.

Be especially watchful in other group settings, like social skills groups. One group that my son was in for NLD and AS kids included a child with ADHD with aggressive behavior. This kid wasn't trying to be bad, and his parents were involved and loving, but he was incredibly confrontational and basically ruined the group with his negativity and manipulative game-playing. This child wasn't consciously trying to be mean – he was simply dealing with life as best as he could given the skills that he had. However, aggressive kids often are anathema to a kid with AS as their manipulative skills mesh a little too seamlessly with the AS tendency toward naiveté.

Social Promotion vs. Repeating a Grade

Controversy rages around this subject, and rightly so, as either scenario can be emotionally damaging to a child if not done properly. The current thinking in the United States seems to be that holding a child back is best done early in the child's academic career – kindergarten through second grade. Beyond that, it can be difficult for any child to accommodate socially to the change. However, a grade change could also help even the field socially, and open up new doors for social interaction your child might not have had before. It depends on the context, the age, the child, and the way the situation is handled.

After second grade the majority of schools will continue to move a child forward, even if there are problems; again, for the good of the child. Social promotion can be damaging if it is covering up a real learning disability, however. If the child's disability is not addressed, it is likely to manifest itself again in the repeated grade.

So, before agreeing to allow your child to be held back (which may otherwise be the best thing to do), find out what the root problems are and make sure that your child will get all of the extra help she may need. Ask for additional testing if need be. If you uncover a learning disability, you may want to ask the school to provide tutoring and other interventions to prevent the child from being held back.

If, however, your child is simply not as mature as the rest of his classmates in all areas, and there is no learning disability, it is probably a good idea to let him be held back. Make sure he understands that this happens to kids all the time, and that it isn't because he is stupid. Point out that smart kids know how to let others help them, and this is a form of getting help.

The School's "Hidden Curriculum"

As part of the discussion about school, we need to bring up the notion of a hidden curriculum. This term has been around for several decades, and was believed to have been coined by the sociologist Philip Jackson in his book *Life in Classrooms* (1968). "Hidden curriculum" refers to the concept that as social institutions, schools not only teach things like mathematics and spelling, but also what society as a whole values and respects – the unspoken rules and regulations to which a given culture (society as a whole or your child's school in particular) expects us to conform.

For example, children where I live, especially boys, are expected to be both highly intelligent and competitive. Mastery is key, and children who are not internally driven to get all "A"s, play several sports and play them well, win awards and trophies, are considered to be slackers or losers.

While other parents and teachers may say that these are not necessarily the trappings of a healthy, well-adjusted child, the hidden agenda in my child's school says otherwise – in an unspoken, but equally compelling way.

More disastrously for children with AS, part of the hidden curriculum extends to conforming to certain behaviors. Sitting up straight in a chair, raising your hand before asking a question, using the bathroom only at recess unless it is an emergency, turning in homework at the beginning of class, writing down assignments in the back of your notebook, smiling politely at the teacher's jokes, praising a classmate's artwork ... the list is endless. Even if your child is on an IEP, and even if the teacher knows that these behaviors are difficult for him, he may still be ostracized for not complying – probably by his peers, and possibly even by the teacher, who may hold an internal, even unconscious, bias against any child who does not conform to these unspoken teacher-pleasing rules.

What can you do? First, look at our culture as a whole, and then look at the culture of your child's school, your community. Understand in an unflinching way what is expected, overtly or not, of your child. You will then need to decide if these unspoken goals – compliance, competitiveness, attractiveness, intelligence, drive – are things you want for your child, or are things that he will need in order to be successful as an adult. Of course, defining what is successful is an interesting undertaking in itself.

If your child is breaking the hidden curriculum at his school, it may be difficult for him to fit in. Try to understand what is expected of him, because he will probably not be able to figure this out on his own. Does he need to appear tidier? Should his homework be laser printed rather than handwritten? Should he bring more "mainstream" items in for share day? Obviously, this is a double-edged sword. On the one hand, we want our children to be individuals and allow them to express themselves for who they are. But if self-expression is breaking the secret rules and causing him to be ostracized from his peers, and possibly singled out as a troublemaker by his teacher, the child will not be a true part of the social fabric he lives in.

I'm not advocating to "redo" your child, but I think that it is important to remember that we all live in a social context of one sort or another, and that we all must modify our behaviors to get along with those around us – sometimes several times a day. Most of us can negotiate the hidden agendas around us without much problem. Your child probably cannot. Figure out the code together, and work out how he can comply in ways that don't threaten or abandon your own values. To help you get started I highly recommend the book *The Hidden Curriculum – Practical Solutions for Understanding Unstated Rules in Social Situations* by Brenda Myles, Melissa Trautman, and Ronda Schelvan (2004). There is even a one-a-day calendar (www.asperger.net), which offers a fun and informal way to work on a hidden curriculum item each day of the year – whether at home or at school.

The good news is that the world of adults seems to be somewhat more forgiving than the world of children in terms of adhering to the hidden curriculum, and in fact many of the strengths our AS kids have (tenacity, high intelligence, detail-oriented) will serve them well as adults in the world outside.

References

Frankel, F., & Wetmore, B. (1996). *Good friends are hard to find*. Los Angeles: Perspective Publishing.

Jackson, P. (1968). *Life in classrooms*. New York: Teachers College Press.

Kranowitz, C. (2006). *The out-of-sync child*. New York: The Berkeley Publishing Group.

Myles, B., Trautman, M., & Schelvan, R. (2004). *The hidden curriculum – Practical solutions for understanding unstated rules in social situations*. Shawnee Mission, KS: Autism Asperger Publishing Company.

Chapter 7

It's a Jungle out There!

The playground can be anything but fun for a kid with AS. As in a real jungle, there are complicated and unspoken laws, pecking orders, and territories. It's survival of the fittest and can be a bewildering place for a child who doesn't easily fit in.

What Happens on the Playground

To most average kids, recess and P.E. are the best times of the school day. The students eagerly line up to get outside and run around. So why is it that so many kids with AS find reasons to stay inside, or dawdle at the door? Recess can be torture for these kids. Children with AS usually thrive on structure and can often handle the classroom fairly well. But left to the unstructured world of the playground, they can fall apart – so many stimuli and so many choices, and so many of them seem beyond your child's abilities.

"Odd" Kid Out

Recess is about playing with friends, organizing a game of pickup basketball, or hanging with the cool kids and yakking about the latest Game Cube cartridge. It's a time when children work on their interactive skills in myriad ways, learning by watching others how the game of social interaction is played.

But for kids with AS, it's a confusing time. Frequently, these kids either play by themselves, swinging or repeatedly climbing the jungle gym, unable to negotiate the social games around them. The heartbreaking part is that many times the AS child wants to play with other kids, but doesn't know how. And, if she steels herself to ask to play a game with others, her attempts to join in are often so awkward that they are rejected.

The playground is also a prime location for bullying, as the children are not under close supervision by adults. This makes children with AS feel even worse about recess, and it's no wonder that many of them would rather play by themselves than be subjected to rejection and humiliation again and again.

"Weak" Kid Out

Not only do kids with AS have weak social skills, they also tend to have weak motor skills, and generally do not excel at sports – a big part of many kids' free time. So, even if your child manages to talk his way into a basketball game, he is still a prime target for bullying and ridicule if he doesn't play well.

So what's a kid to do? He's likely to head back to the swing set or the library where he feels safe. While these are good alternatives some of the time, as a full-time strategy they don't help him learn the social skills that he needs to be successful in life.

Everyone Looks Forward to Recess, Right?

By now, you've gotten the picture that many children with AS want to avoid recess altogether, and you'd be right. The problem is that you may not realize just how bad the situation is, because your child may hide his feelings, or be unaware of them.

When Will was in kindergarten, recess was awful. He could never seem to get to a tricycle before they were all taken, the swings were the domain of four little girls who always ran ahead of everyone else, and the jungle gym was the setting for a raucous game of tag, which was too much for him. The teachers told me that he often hung out to the side of these activities, never joining in. So, we worked together to encourage Will to play with at least one other child each day. At school, the teacher would find another child for Will to play with and encourage them to play.

This went on for a week, with some success, until Will started to act out in class. In kindergarten, the punishment for misbehavior in class was missing recess. Hopefully, you're a little more sharp than we were and can see more quickly than we did that Will was misbehaving in class so that he would have to miss recess and, therefore, miss the agonizing social interaction. It took us two weeks and three trips to the principal's office before we figured it out! We adjusted the plan a bit, telling Will that he only needed to play three times a week. Also, the teachers broke up the swing set cartel, enabling Will to swing (a favorite past time) the other days.

You may notice that your child has found similar behaviors to get her out of social situations. In general, kids who don't like recess tend to melt down in class either right before or right after recess, often when they are lining up (and before the teacher gets there to monitor the students). Look for related causes. You may find that the social aspects of her day are causing her a great deal of anxiety.

Asking Questions

The best way to find out what's happening at recess and in P.E. is to ask your child. Don't expect much from a general question like, "So, how was recess?" because you're likely to get the standard "Fine." Instead, ask questions that encourage the child to open up:

> *"Who did you play with at recess?"*
>
> *"What did you do at recess?"*
>
> *"What games are you learning in P.E.?"*
>
> *"If you could play any game, what would it be?"*
>
> *"I bet Shauna would like to play jump rope. What would it be like to ask her?"*

In general, asking open-ended questions (questions that cannot be answered with a simple yes or no) yields more fruitful conversational grist than closed-ended questions. Finding out what is happening and what your child would like to be doing gives you some leverage to start building your child's skills.

Building Alliances

Building alliances here means creating both adult and child alliances. Find out who the playground supervisors are during recess and lunch hour. If they seem approachable, ask them to keep an eye on your child. You can explain that he has been having a hard time finding someone to play with and that you'd like to know how he's doing. Most parents and teachers are more than happy to report back their findings.

Further, building alliances with other parents helps you find the other children who have similar issues, or children who are mellow and would make suitable playmates. You can also ask your child's teacher. In kindergarten, a parent I know asked the teacher to suggest a friend for her son. The children are now both in high school and are still good friends. Once you discover these kids, you can encourage your child to seek them out at playtime and ask them to play.

Cheap Tricks for the Playground

If you've discovered that your child hates recess and lunch because of his lack of social finesse, you'll need to find a way to help him out. Don't underestimate the importance of this social time. While it's fine to let your child decompress and be alone some of the time, he needs positive social interactions to be a self-sufficient adult, and that's our job, remember? Also, if any of the programs mentioned below don't exist at your child's school, ask if you can start one. Maybe you could just do one lunch hour a week, but it will make a huge difference to your child as well as his peers.

✋ Library

Many schools now offer library programs at lunch for kids who don't like to roll around in the mud playing touch football. The library is a good place for kids who can't handle the raucous stimulation of the playground. If your school has a library program, tell your child about it and encourage him to participate one or two days a week.

Library time is also a good time and place to let students finish homework or schoolwork that they could not complete in time elsewhere, especially for older kids who can do the work with little intervention and support. I caution you about having your child go there every single day, though, as that may reinforce his hiding from other kids and won't get him the exercise he likely needs.

✋ Clubs and Special Interest Groups

Like library, special interest clubs give children a way to interact with other children in a structured environment. At our school, we've been blessed with myriad options, from chorus on Fridays, to juggling clubs and chess clubs throughout the week.

The school also offers what they call the "Linus and Lucy Table," which is a cart loaded with board games such as Battleship, Yahtzee, and the like. This cart is brought out to a quiet area of the playground by sixth-grade volunteers, and the kids check out the games at the beginning of recess and check them back in at the end. This arrangement is immensely popular with all sorts of kids, and is extremely easy to set up. Speak to your principal about this idea if you think it would benefit your child, and then organize a "game drive" where parents can donate games from a list.

Finally, you can ask to start a special interest group yourself, whether it's puppet shows for littler kids or origami for older kids (great for developing fine-motor skills). If your child has a need and an interest, there is surely another child in the school with the same needs. Help fill it!

✋ Computer Lab

Like the library, the computer lab may be open during recess or lunchtime, and this can provide another landing place for your child. Some schools have educational games children can play, as well as educational software they may use to do their schoolwork. Also, like the library, this may be a good time and place for your child to finish any undone homework, or to get more practice in keyboarding (which can be a very useful skill for children with poor handwriting).

Although your child might find other children with similar interests, computer lab and the library should not be used every day as they both tend to encourage solitary, rather than social, activities.

✋ Teaching Your Child Easy Games

One of the easiest ways to get your child to participate in playground games it to make sure that he understands the games that the kids play and gets some private practice in playing them.

Find out what games your child is interested in and find out what games are currently popular among his peers, and if need be, find out how to play these games. Then, take the time to teach your child how to play them, or better yet, see if you can find a tolerant kid who will teach him the game after school one day. Because kids with Asperger Syndrome have low frustration tolerance, often have low self-esteem, and process information differently or more slowly than others, they can rarely watch a game, learn how to play, and jump in. Teaching your child the game directly is the first step.

✋ Teaching Your Child How to Ask to Join In

The second step, after mastering the sought-after game, is to teach your child how to enter an ongoing game. You can enlist your team of experts to help (such as his teacher, classroom aide, and so forth) to help with this training. While learning how to enter a game may seem like the simplest thing in the world (especially if you yourself are socially adept and were so as a child), to an AS kid it is a baffling ritual.

The best book that I have found that describes how kids enter a game is Good Friends Are Hard to Find by Fred Frankel and Barry Wetmore (1996), but in short, here's how it works.

Boys tend to watch a game from the sidelines for a bit, not too close to be in the way, but close enough for the players to get the idea that they want to play. After a few minutes, the boy asks if he can play on the losing side. The boys generally let the new child play.

Girls, on the other hand, tend to watch from the sidelines and figure out who the "queen bee" is – usually there is a dominant girl whose jump rope they are using, or who is making the rules for the game. After figuring out who the dominant girl is, the new girl will ask her directly if she can join in.

I bet you didn't know this, did you? Neither did I! And yet, non-Asperger kids learn these confounding rules all the time and never even know it.

Given this information, your job is to explain all of this to your child, and do some role-playing about how he can ask to join in a game. Help him find the right words – and the right tone of voice – to ask kids if he can play. Then, when he seems to be comfortable with the idea, tell him that you'd like him to try it at recess the next day. Get him to check in with you at the end of the day and tell you how it went. You may find, as I did, that it will take several days of gentle goading before he will steel up the nerve to do it, but with love, praise, and encouragement, he will probably try before long.

So, what happens if your child makes a bid to play with the other kids and is rejected? Sadly, it will happen, so prepare your child and yourself ahead of time. In fact, fear of rejection will likely be one of the reasons why your child won't want to try. If he asks, "What happens if they say I can't play?" my recommendation is to tell him to put on his happiest face, say brightly, "Okay!" and walk away. If he cries or complains to the kids, he will only further ostracize himself.

Then, have him try the next day or another day the same week. Tell him that he needs to try three times to join in a game (try to make sure it's the same game with the same kids). If after three tries the children still do not let him play, tell your child that you will speak to the principal because all schools have a policy of no shut-outs. To not let a child play is just not fair.

It's very important to model standing up for what is right. I urge you not to let this go and allow your child to slide back into the "no one likes me" mode without intervention. Your child should not be shut out of games. If this is happening at your school, notify the principal. All children need to be taught tolerance and kindness for others, and all children need to be taught when it is appropriate to stand up and say, "This is not okay."

Once you are over this hurdle (if you should face it), make sure your child is playing by the rules and enjoying himself. Check in on a regular basis with him.

✋ After-School Scaffolding

In some areas, the playground is a hotbed of activity after school. If your school is one such place, and if your schedule allows it, let your child hang out a little after school with the other kids and play. This is a good way to segue into a spontaneous playdate, or just get a little more social skills practice. If other mothers stay around watching their kids, it's also great way to meet other parents and see the kids in action. Even if you work full time, maybe once or twice a month you can leave work early (or take an extra-late lunch) so that you can be there with your child and get a taste of her social world.

Watch your child, and learn how she interacts. Watch the other children, and learn how they interact. This is a great way to see what areas your child needs to work on, and while you're there, you can whisper some advice and encouragement to her in the moment.

✋ Packing the Right Lunch

Yes, you read that right. Pack the right lunch! We are getting into what I call "the cool factor" now, and unless you are on a strict Vegan diet or your child has food allergies, I highly recommend taking a look at the contents of your child's lunch to see what it says about him. You are what you eat, right?

So, let him eat "cool foods," at least some of the time. For example, a kid who eats egg salad sandwiches and Fig Newtons every single day, unless utterly cool in other ways, is bound to be labeled an uncool kid. How about packing a cool snack that he can share with someone, like fruit rollups or Reese's Pieces? Maybe your child loves sushi. It may be a bit odd, but it's still cool (just remember to pack it well in cold packs so it stays fresh). Lunchables, while questionable nutritionally, definitely have a cool factor. Once a month, will it really kill him? No. But it will make him look like a "regular" kid. Ditto an occasional (once a week or so) blue applesauce, Gogurts, Krispy Kreme Donuts, what have you.

As long as you aren't forcing your kid to eat things he doesn't like, and you aren't abandoning any tightly held food tenets and are keeping his overall diet nutritionally sound, think about what other kids see in your child's lunchbox. Also, think about what other kids like to eat – and maybe pack an extra in your child's lunch so that he can share. The way to a boy's heart (and the road to a budding friendship) may be a Krispy Kreme Donut.

Of course, some AS kids have some very rigid ideas about what they will eat and what they won't eat. One kid I know would eat nothing but bread if given the choice, and nothing green or squishy would ever pass over his lips. Lots of non-Asperger children have strange food likes and dislikes, but their peers will likely tolerate these quirks. An AS kid is a bit more difficult. He is already at a social disadvantage, and helping him work through some of his more bizarre eating habits will help him fit in a bit better. Just don't push it – most doctors and child psychologists will warn you to not get into pitched battles over food.

✋ Wearing the Right Clothes

Still in the cool category, which is also part of the "hidden curriculum," we move on to what your child is wearing. This one can be tricky for a couple of reasons. First off, many kids with AS have definite hypersensitivity to the way clothes feel – too tight, too loose, too bumpy, too smooth. And once you find clothes that your child will wear, it's easy to buy seven of them in different colors and call it done.

But as with the lunch, your child makes an impression by what he wears, and it is very important that he looks as much as possible like the other kids. I don't mean that you should spend $150 on Air Jordans, or that he should be decked out tip-to-toe in Abercrombie and Fitch regalia. What I mean is that your child should be wearing clothes that neither stand out for their flashiness nor stand out for their unhipness. Look at the children in his class, take the kids in the middle and use them as a guide. Remember, you will have to do the legwork here. If you ask your child what the kids at school are wearing, he'll likely report, "clothes" and nothing more.

At age 10, my son loved elastic waistbands, but was in men's sizes. I couldn't let him wear sweat pants year 'round, and it's hard (but not impossible) to find elastic waistband shorts for a tall kid. It's important to make sure your kid looks like a typical kid, neither too old nor too young for his grade. It may sound petty, but it's important. The same goes for haircuts, bikes, scooters, and the like. You don't need to spoil your child with extravagant gifts, but do make sure he has the necessary stuff to mark him "normal" in his social group.

✋ Keeping Your Child Clean

It can be challenging enough to keep any boy clean, but given the seeming fear or aversion of soap and water that many kids with AS have, it can be a nightmare keeping them looking like they belong to the human race. When Will was about 6, I dubbed him "the human napkin" because he could not stop himself from wiping his ketchup-y face on the shoulder of his t-shirt.

As much of a battle as this is, it's important and one not to be overlooked. Help keep your child looking kempt by insisting on showers, toothbrushing, and hair combing. Put it on a chore chart at home if you need to, and find work-arounds when necessary. For example, short haircuts mean no hair brushing – problem solved! Remind your child at home to use his napkin, then pack a napkin in his lunch. If the napkin comes home dirty (yippee!), give him a reward. Don't let him wear dirty clothes to school, and get him to regularly wash his hands. All of this may sound pedantic, but the last thing your child needs is to have the label "pig pen" on top of everything else. This gets more difficult as they hit puberty, so hang on.

✋ A Word About GameBoys, Nintendos, and Computer Games

One of the most hotly debated topics with regard to AS kids (and children in general) is whether or not to let them have access to video games. This is a tough one for a couple of reasons. On one hand, kids with AS tend to be solitary, proficient at computers, and when truly involved, can focus really well on something, making GameBoys and the like a natural fit. Additionally, video games increase hand-eye coordination, visual acuity, and fine-motor skills. Depending on the game, they can also build problem-solving skills, increase vocabulary and inference skills, logic, and mathematics. These games are also definitely cool in most circles, and a child who is very proficient in a currently cool game is considered with some reverence by his peers. All of these are weighty considerations for our kids.

On the other hand, video games in general enforce noninteractional play, even when the game is for more than one person (the kids are playing with the game, not with each other, and the rules are very set, so there is little if any social interaction). Kids with AS also, with their tendency to fixation, can block out the entire universe for days on end if allowed to indulge in video games. This can lead to problems, like carpal tunnel syndrome, headaches, and lack of exercise. For these socially isolated kids, it also keeps them from building their weak areas of gross-motor skills, social interaction, and imaginative play.

My recommendation is to allow video games – sometimes. I don't see the harm in a kid doing something he really, really likes, and to get proficient enough at it so that he acquires a bit of the "cool factor," but it is definitely to his detriment to let him play to the exclusion of other activities. What I do, and many parents I know do the same, is to set a limit, like allowing use in the car or in the dentist's office or after all his homework and chores are done on a week night before dinner. This keeps the peace. I also insist that all games be age-appropriate and as nonviolent as possible. When the games (or the whining) get out of control, the games go in the closet.

Working with Coaches, P.E. Teachers, and Playground Monitors

As mentioned earlier, children with AS usually have a distinctive lack of interest and/or ability in sports, due to their low gross- and fine-motor skills, inability to process information quickly in a relatively unstructured setting, and low social skills.

This does not mean that these kids are destined to lives as couch potatoes, but it does mean that they may need some help from older children and adults to bolster these skills. And because exercise and movement is critical to the overall health of any child, you may need to be proactive here to make sure your child stays fit. This can be a battle.

Asking Your Child Who Can Help

One of the best ways to find allies for your child is to ask him who at school is friendly and fun and knows a lot about sports. This may be the P.E. teacher, a parent who helps out with P.E., or a playground monitor who is always helping kids start games. If your child can't identify someone, ask your child's teacher.

If your school has a great P.E. teacher (as we are fortunate to have), see if you can catch him on the playground some day and ask if he would be willing to give a little extra attention to your child. Whether or not you tell this person that your child has AS is up to you. Even though federal law mandates that anyone working with your child should know that he is on an IEP, the truth of the matter is that the coach may not know formally, but probably knows intuitively, that your child has some deficits in this area.

If you are able to build a rapport with this person and he seems genuinely interested in helping, ask if he can recommend any local programs or coaches who would be willing to work with your child to build her expertise and comfort in sports and physical activities. Merely asking the question does several things. First, it tells the coach that you are interested in seeking help and that you want to be an ally in your child's physical fitness. This in itself tends to have the magical effect of prompting the coach to look after your child a bit – giving her lots of praise and encouragement, checking in with her more frequently to see how she's doing, and so forth. It also puts the coach (or playground monitor or whomever) on alert to keep an eye on your child and to encourage her to join a game or try something new.

Finally, you may find that the coach either has contacts he can share with you or ideas that you can try at home to encourage physical activity. Many formally trained P.E. teachers have taken some occupational or physical therapy classes, and have great ideas on how to get your child involved.

It's a good idea to make an alliance with whoever is watching the kids at recess, and ask if they can keep an eye on your child to see if he is playing with other children, interacting and so on, or if he is hanging on the sides. If you find that your child is not engaging as much as you think he could be, the monitor can occasionally nudge him into an interactive game. Having an ally on the playground is very beneficial to your child as well, because it affords him a sense of being protected and gives him someone to go to if things go wrong.

References

Frankel, F., & Wetmore, B. (1996). *Good friends are hard to find*. Los Angeles: Perspective Publishing.

Gray, C. (2002). *The sixth sense II*. New York: Free Spirit Publishing.

Chapter 8

Making Friends

One of the hardest aspects of your AS child's life is to make friends – one, two, or three good friends he can count on to be there for him. Everyone needs that feeling of "sharedness" and bonding that comes from having a close friend, and your child needs this closeness as much, if not more, than others.

I recommend you spend a fair amount of time in pursuit of friendship for your child. Setting up positive experiences now will pay huge dividends later. Through friendships, he will gain the ability to relate to others in meaningful ways – at college, at work, and later in a committed relationship and with his own children.

It's great to support your child at home, for him to be close to his siblings, and to get part of his social interaction from his nuclear and extended family. However, family is no substitute for the ability to go out into the world and generate and sustain meaningful relationships with others.

Fully functioning adults have friendships, relationships, love affairs, and marriages. Start now. It takes years of practice for all people to master these relationships, and if you think your child will figure it out later you're likely to be mistaken, to the detriment of your child.

The Heartbreak Starts Here

As important as learning how to be a friend is for your child, expect it to be an uneven road – sometimes it will be smooth going, and at other times you'll hit pothole after pothole. That's okay. Like everything else in life, learning how to be a friend is a process, not a destination.

Everyone Got Invited ... Except Me

As your child begins to observe the social interactions of those around her, she will begin to realize that she is different. She may see that other children often have playdates and that she doesn't. She may observe how children pair up, group up, and pal around, and how she is not part of that social milieu. You are also likely to have to bear witness to your child's heartbreak when she comes home with a story about how everyone got invited to someone's birthday party, swim party, or sleepover, except her (kids with AS are often masters of the "everyone," "always," and "never" overgeneralized statements).

While it is a small consolation to know that not "everyone" actually got invited to a given party, the truth probably is that your child isn't being invited to as many parties as others, and that she may never be. Further, your child is smart enough to know she isn't being invited, and this can cause her great pain.

You can do several things to combat this situation and make sure that your child gets invited to at least some of the parties and events she wants to go to.

Coping with Your Own Heartbreak

Before we jump into the tactics of how to get your child involved with other kids and begin to build friendships, let's stop for a moment and talk about you. A parent's reactions and emotions are rarely talked about in books such as these, yet I think it is a vital part of the picture.

Like most parents, I take it very personally when my child is excluded. Because my child is a part of me in a very real way, his rejection feels personal, like I am the one being rejected. Further, because we are the mentors of our children, it can feel as if our parenting abilities are called into question when our children are not deemed "good enough" to attend a much-ballyhooed party. These feelings are very normal, and I recommend you spend some time thinking about your feelings or talking with your spouse or a close friend about them.

It is hard to witness your child's pain and frustration. It is probably one of the hardest things you do as a parent. Acknowledge it for what it is, and then try to channel the hurt into productive energy for your child.

Finding the Teaching Moments

Along with coping with your own feelings, another way to build "psychic wellness" into your family is to make sure to take advantage of teaching moments. Using the example above, let's say your child comes home in tears because he didn't get invited to Sam's party, and "everyone else did."

"Really?" you ask. "Everyone else in third grade got invited?"

"Yes, everyone!" retorts your teary child.

Mom hauls out the third-grade phone list.

"Let's see. Jimmy?"

"Yep."

"John?"

"Yep; he's the one who told me."

"Susan?"

"No, Susan is a girl, duh!"

"Okay, so the girls didn't get invited."

"Right."

"So, not everyone in third grade."

"Well, duh, Mom, the girls didn't get invited."

"Okay, what about Philip?"

"Well, not Philip because Jimmy and John don't like him."

"Uh-huh. Well, what about Suresh?"

"No, not Suresh either, but like, just about everyone else!"

"So, okay, some kids, maybe even a lot of kids got invited, but not all. And you were part of the 'not all' kids who didn't get invited, right?"

"Right."

"And that really hurts."

"Yeah. I wanted to go really bad because they're going to play mini-golf."

"Yeah, that's disappointing. Would you like to try to be friends with Jimmy?"

"No, not really; he's kind of a brat, but John is nice."

"Well, then let's see if you can start being friends with John, how would that be?"

So, the teaching moments here are to:

❒ Help your child see that "never," "always," "everyone," and "no one" statements are generally false and self-defeating

❒ Validate your child's sadness

❒ Encourage your child to turn the situation around and work on it (here, by identifying someone new he'd like to try to be friends with)

Other teaching moments that may present themselves include learning how to identify different levels of friendships, and to identify how friends move in and out of these varying levels. This is something that kids generally learn on their own, but that AS kids often have a hard time with. Look at the illustration below.

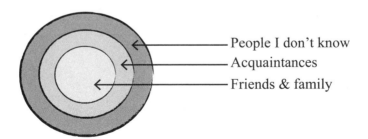

People I don't know
Acquaintances
Friends & family

I used this target picture to demonstrate to Will the varying levels of friendship and explained that it describes everyone's levels of friends, not just his. Starting from the middle are the people he knows and trusts and calls friends. When he told me "I don't have any friends," I made him write down the people who are, in fact, his friends, such as Alex, Justin, and Marci. I explained to him that most people only have a small group of really good friends at any time, and I listed the people to whom I am especially close, to illustrate – four or five people. This helps him to see himself as typical given the larger social context.

We then moved over to the acquaintance group. Here we talked about the kids at school with whom he was friendly, but with whom he didn't have playdates or other deeper social contact. I then listed the people whom I am acquainted with. At this point, it's useful to describe how throughout a lifetime, friends and acquaintances sometimes trade places. Your child might have been particularly close to a kid in first grade, but now they just say "Hi" to each other. Emphasize that this is normal. You can also talk about how friends sometimes argue or disagree, and can move to the acquaintance circle for a bit until the friendship is repaired. Be prepared with an example of your own – this helps your child to understand that this is a common process.

Finally, we moved to the outer circle – this is the rest of the world with which the child is not yet acquainted. When things are particularly bad, it can be reassuring to know that there are lots of people he hasn't met yet – his best friend might be just around the corner waiting for him!

The other thing that this illustration is useful for is to explain why it's inappropriate to invite someone from the acquaintance group to a sleepover, and how acquaintances become friends slowly, with repeated contact until they move fully into the friends' circle.

Teaching Your Child How to Be Thoughtful

While this is a rather broad heading, there are specific things you can do to teach your child how to be a thoughtful friend, all of which will pay off handsomely as she reaches adulthood.

Teach Her to Say "Please," "Thank You," and "You're Welcome"

It is important that children learn how to say "please" and "thank you," yet there millions of little kids who apparently have never been taught this skill. It's far more than just uttering the words – it's the feeling behind it that matters. Help instill a sense of gratitude in your child by reminding her to say "please" and "thank you," especially before she heads out the door to a party or other social function. Then, check with her to see if she remembered. If she didn't, that's okay; just remind her again. Remind her when you're with her and make sure you model this behavior yourself, always using "please" and "thank you" when interacting with others. The world is a lot kinder to people who take the time to appreciate what others have done for them.

Teach Her to Say "I'm Sorry"

It seems to be difficult to teach children with AS to take responsibility for their actions when the actions were not intentional. For example, you may have no problem getting your child to apologize for socking her sister in the arm, but she may have a very difficult time understanding why she should apologize for stepping on her foot – she didn't mean it, after all! Nevertheless, it is important that all children understand that they are responsible for all of their actions, intended or not. Model this behavior, but also remind the child to say she's sorry if you catch her in the moment. I have even gone so far as to have my son call up another child and apologize on the phone, rather than let an "I'm sorry" go unsaid.

Teach Her How to Write a Card, Letter, or Email

While your child may never be a master at social writing, by second or third grade, she can master a simple thank-you note to someone who was kind to her or to children who gave her birthday presents. If she won't sit still long enough to make a card or write a letter, let her use email. She may find that this is a great way to stay in touch, and as long as it is social communication of some form, it's worth-while. If she still resists, ask a favorite friend or relative who lives far away to write your child, inviting her to write back. They can put the teaser in, "If you write me a letter, I promise to write you another one back." Most kids are so thrilled to get mail of any sort that this might prompt your child to start up written correspondence for a while.

Teach Her How to Buy a Gift

Children with AS are notoriously bad at purchasing appro-priate gifts for friends and families, and if left to their own devices, will likely select something that they want them-selves. One mother once told me that if she had let him, her son would gladly have purchased a refrigerator for his father for Father's Day, as refrigerators were his latest passion.

Start by going alone with your child (if at all possible) to the toy store. Before you even enter the store, make it clear that you are there to buy a present for her friend, and not for her. Have her think about what her friend likes to do: sports, Legos, Pokémon, what? This may take a little do-ing, and if your child is young or has a very difficult time "reading" other kids, you may want to call the other child's parents in advance and get suggestions. Once you have decided on two or three themes, take your child into the store. Give her a price range and begin looking at different possibilities. If you do this frequently enough, your child will begin to learn how to pick appropriate gifts for friends and family, and you may be able to let her pick out gifts without any intervention. Also, make sure she learns how to wrap a present, even if it's just putting it in a gift bag.

Teach Her How to Cheer up a Friend

Because kids with AS lack empathy, they may have a hard time recognizing when a friend or acquaintance is in need of support. Begin by pointing out situations where someone looks like they could use cheering up. You can point out characters on TV or in books who are having a rough time, and stop and ask your child, "Gee, do you think that person is sad?" Once your child has begun to read the emotional state of those around her, you can encourage her to be a good friend. You can start by asking, "If you were having as bad a day as that person, what would you want a friend to say to you?" By framing the question in terms of your child's own perception, she can make a better guess about what others might want. Then, when you're with your child in a social situation and see someone she knows whose feelings are hurt or who got bumped on the playground, encourage your child to go over and offer support. This might take a bit of nudging, and your child may be rebuffed initially. That's okay. Learning when and how to lend a hand to a friend is key. The rest just takes practice.

Teach Her How to Be a Champion to Others

Asperger children are often the brunt of bullying from other kids, but they are by no means the only children who get bullied on the playground or in other social situations. As part of bully-proofing your child, consider encouraging her to advocate for other children who get bullied. This doesn't mean teaching her to belt someone who teases a friend, but to stand by a friend who is being harassed. Using the same techniques she would use when she is the target, your child can walk up to her friend and ask her to go with her to play somewhere else and leave the bully in the dust. Bullies tend to lose interest in children who won't play their game, and if your child not only refuses to be provoked but aids others in learning this skill, the bullies are likely to leave her alone. And, your child will have learned a very important lesson in friendship.

Building Alliances

One of the best ways to help your child make friends is to find the likeliest kids. Generally, but not always, tolerant kids come with tolerant parents, and vice versa. Going to PTA meetings, school events, and the like, are great ways to find tolerant parents.

What Others May See in Your Child

As you are building alliances within your community, it's a good idea to be mindful of what others see in your child. While adults, as well as older and younger children, often find AS kids to be precocious, warm, and witty, their age peers almost invariably see them as nerds or geeks. This seems to be because children instinctively know what the parameters of "normal" behavior are for themselves and their peers. Any peer who acts outside of these parameters, even subtly, therefore, appears odd or out of sync. Older and younger children and adults often don't apply this peer measuring stick to their AS friend, and may be delighted by their funny behavior. (Some non-peers, of course, can also be annoyed.) For this reason, you may notice that your AS child prefers kids a few years younger or older than he is.

Parents and other adults are often another story, and this is both a blessing and a curse for you and your child. Because many children with AS present relatively normally to the casual observer and because they tend to gravitate toward adults and engage them in conversation, parents may think that your kid is the sweetest, smartest thing they've ever met. That is, until their own child comes home with a broken binder and a story about how your child stomped on it because there was a drawing of spiders on it and he is mortally afraid of spiders.

If an incident such as this occurs, sadly, less tolerant parents will probably side with their child and may tell him to stay away from your child. If the parents are unaware that your child has a real disorder, your parenting ability will be called into question, adding insult to injury.

It is painful to first see your child being alienated and then be alienated yourself. The good news is that not all parents are intolerant. Some insightful parents will have figured out on their own that your child may have special challenges, and if you stay active in your child's school, you are nearly guaranteed to find some wonderful parents as allies.

Finding Tolerant Parents and Children

A word about tolerance. I think we'd all like to think that we are tolerant, accepting people, but the truth of the matter is that none of us is without prejudice. Because we are not without prejudice, we can hardly expect the rest of the world to be, so remember to start at home with your tolerance campaign. Once you have found other tolerant parents (or kids, specifically), try to find out what that child likes – video games, Pokémon cards, playing miniature golf, and so on. Once you have identified possible likes and dislikes, work with your child to structure an outing or playdate that the other child will like. Then, extend the invitation. (See the section below for more information.) When teaching and promoting tolerance, you may also want to consider older or younger playmates for your child. There are no laws saying that your child can only play with age peers. As mentioned, often children older and younger than your child are more tolerant of your child's differences than children of his age. When pairing an AS kid with a younger child, you may also be able to glean the benefit of your child being in a mentor or helper role, one that many kids with AS enjoy as they are often very eager to please and assist.

Additionally, getting a mentor/friend for your child can be very beneficial, as these kids need all of the modeling they can get, especially if you can find someone in his or her early 20s or 30s who can help teach your child to be "cool." These friendship skills can be built into peer relationships in the future.

Finding Parents of Kids with Special Needs

Another great way to find potential playmates for your child is to find the other kids in your area who have similar challenges. Kids with AS seem to have an immediate affinity for other AS and NLD kids, and this affinity can develop into a close relationship.

Search the school and local area for other AS kids. You can find them by discreetly asking around, asking your child who is in speech class with him, and joining Friend's Clubs for similarly challenged children. While it may seem less than optimal to generate a friendship with a child who lives 20 miles away, remember that success breeds success. Once your child has had one or two successful friendships, other friendships, maybe even with the kids down the street, will be much easier to build and sustain.

Setting up Short-Duration Playdates

Once you have identified a potential playmate, then what? Here are some guidelines:

❏ For children younger than 8, parents should set up the playdate.

❏ For children older than 8, children can set up the playdate themselves, if they have sufficient phone skills. Role-playing phone calls is useful.

❏ Keep the playdate short; 1.5 hours for younger children and 2.5 hours for older children (playdates can get longer after your child gets comfortable).

❏ Plan activities and snacks with your child before the playdate. Have three different play options for the children, and let them decide which one they want to do.

❏ Talk about how a playdate should go: The doorbell rings, your child answers it, welcomes the friend, invites him in, and so on. Talk about what will happen if the children can't agree on something or what happens if one child gets bored with the activity they are doing. Suggest to your child that if the kids can't agree on what to do, they take turns, each deciding on an activity and staying with it for 15 minutes, and then moving on to another activity. Tell your child that the friend gets to pick first. Role-playing is a good idea here, to ensure that your child has ample opportunity to try these interaction skills first-hand.

❏ Also talk about what will happen if either child gets out of hand; for example, if the children argue about everything, or if one of them hits the other. Tell your child in no uncertain terms that these behaviors will be cause for the playdate to be over, and that you will call the other child's parents and ask them to pick up their child. Then follow through if necessary.

Once the other child shows up and the kids have decided what they want to do, leave the room. You can stay in the area – you can even eavesdrop – but you must give your child some space. If things fall apart, you can intervene gently, perhaps suggesting another activity or a snack. If things really get out of hand, end the playdate and suggest that the children try to play together again another time.

After the playdate, no matter how it went, sit down with your child and review what happened. This is a great way to reinforce all that went well, and talk about what areas might need a little attention. Again, role-playing can be helpful here. Make sure you pay attention to social graces such as "please" and "thank you," turn taking, and negotiating. These are as much keystones to a successful playdate as what the kids actually play together. Even if the other child did not enjoy the selected activity, he will remember that your child was pleasant and may accept another invitation in the future.

Encouraging Your Child to Interact with Others Each Day

For children who have very limited social skills, asking them to play or interact with other children on their own each day might be a little like asking them to walk over hot coals. All of us need some impetus to stretch a bit, and your child is no different.

If your child has little or no interaction with other children during recess or lunchtime, start slowly. Set a goal for your child to ask another child to play, or to join in a game others are playing, at least once a week. Be a strategist: Figure out who your child will approach, or what game he wants to join, and then role play his interactions – joining the child or game, playing the game, ending the game. Also, be sure to talk to your child about the possibility of being rejected.

After your child has a few successful interactions with other children (with practice and patience, he will), increase the number of times a week he interacts with kids. Be mindful that if he is stressed during class time, he may need some time alone to decompress, so don't make a big deal of it if he misses a session or two. Similarly, don't insist that he spend each recess in the company of others unless he enjoys it. Some people need quiet time, and your child may be one of them.

Cheap Tricks for Friendships

There are some things that you can do to make your child more enticing as a potential friend. Do what is reasonable and feasible for you and your family, but don't try to make your family or child something it or he is not.

✋ Being a Cool Parent and Having a Cool House

"Cool" is a relative term, of course, and being a cool parent doesn't mean that you let 6-year-olds scooter in the street without helmets, or let adolescents have access to the beer in your fridge. Instead, being a cool parent means that you aren't overly strict or hovering, that you let kids work things out on their own when possible, and that you allow at least some age-appropriate shenanigans. It also means that you encourage kids to play, make a mess, get dirty or wet, be goofy, and still invite them back.

Along with being a cool parent, you'll want to have a cool house where the children can play. This means that you have at least one totally cool game that everyone is talking about, that you have materials on hand for an impromptu lemonade stand, bubble fest, chalk art gallery, obstacle course, or whatever. You get extra points if you have (and let the kids use) an ice cream maker, trampoline, swimming pool, pool table, or something else that is likely to draw kids to your house.

This may sound like over-commercialism or bribery, but it isn't. It's just common sense. If your 10-year-old invites a friend over to play Lite-Brite, the playdate will run afoul unless the other kid also has a passion for Lite-Brites or can figure out a way to hook it up to the TV and create a multimedia show with it. You don't have to spend a fortune to have a cool house, just imagination. If your child hooks up with someone with a vivid imagination, that's great – say yes to as many ideas as possible to reinforce imaginative play. Worry about the rug another day.

✋ Creating a Cool Environment – For a Day

One of the best ideas I ever had (if I do say so myself) was to host mini-summer camps in our backyard. Will and I picked out eight themes, from water to cooking to mad science, and then I came up with several activities (physical, paper-based, hands-on, etc.) and created a half-day camp around each theme. Then we sent off invitations to all the boys in Will's grade, and told them that if they were free for summer fun, to pick three activities that appealed to them. When I got the responses, I selected dates, and notified the kids which days we were having which camps.

Each camp cost me between $5 and $15 total, for between three and eight kids. We did all eight camps, and each was a success. From this experience, Will made four really good friends with whom he had previously had very little contact. Was it worth it? You bet!

Obviously, you don't have to be an insane type-A like I was and do eight camps – I was a stay-at-home mom with just one child at the time. But you could do a weekend theme camp once in a while, a theme sleepover, or whatever. Try to include children whom you think your child might like but hasn't spent much time with yet. Also, try to pair kids with themes that you know they would like.

This may sound like a lot of work, but it doesn't have to be. First, a themed playdate or day camp gives structure to a social situation, which is what many kids with AS need. Second, your child is the star as it is his home turf, and this may give him a little extra confidence in a social situation. Finally, it helps to build the impression in other children's and parents' minds that you are an involved parent who knows how to have fun and are willing to share that skill with other kids.

The social payoffs are huge for your child, and you just might "match-make" a great friendship.

✋ Being Willing to Accept No "Invite-Backs"

Let's say that your child has been successful in building a few close friendships, and he is now confident enough to call these friends and invite them over for playdates and sleepovers, and that they are generally amenable to coming over. That's fabulous! However, you may notice that your child is not invited back to other children's houses as frequently as you invite them to your house.

Yet proper etiquette calls for a fair trade of playdates, where roughly one playdate at your house will generate a playdate at the other child's house. This is great in theory, but in practice, it may not happen. For better or worse, while other children may be more than happy to come to your house to play with your child, they may not reciprocate and invite her back as frequently – or ever.

Some parents take great offense at this, and stop inviting a child over to play if the playdates are not reciprocated. Frankly, I think this is cutting off your nose to spite your face. In a perfect world your child would be invited to other children's houses time and time again, but this may not be the way it works out. I encourage you to overlook this aspect, unless you truly believe you and your child are being taken advantage of. It is far better to ensure that your child has adequate and successful play experience with other children than to worry about being "even-steven."

Once your child has buddied up with one or two children, and if you have gotten to know the parents at all, it's not outrageous to ask them on occasion if your child could come over and play at their house. Don't make it sound like babysitting by saying, "I've got a dentist appointment on Tuesday, could Bobby come over "(unless you know the parents well and this is okay with them). Instead, you can say something like, "I'm wondering if Bobby could come over some day this week and play with Greg – I've got my hands full this week, and Bobby would love to see your son." Most parents are more than happy to oblige if they are given some freedom as to when they have your child over and it is for a reasonable length of time.

What Happens When Someone Takes Advantage of Your Child

From time to time, some child might insinuate herself into your child's life and take advantage of her. This can manifest in several ways, from taunting, to bullying, to coercion, to out-and-out extortion.

This is an exceptionally painful situation, because AS and NLD kids tend to be socially naïve and may not realize that someone is taking advantage of them. They may only report feeling bad about a situation, if they register it as incorrect behavior at all.

Some children, like adults, seem to thrive on having power over others, and because of your child's inability to fully register social rules, she is a prime target for children who need to manipulate others to feel good about themselves.

Because your child may not have the tools to understand that she is being taken advantage of, keep in constant communication with her about her daily life to head off a full-blown catastrophe.

Finding the Teaching Moments

Early in the fifth grade, Will told me that three kids (all relatively new to the school) were teasing him and an NLD kid at school, interrupting games that they were playing with other friends by using a divide-and-conquer approach and calling them "spazzes" and "geeks" in front of the other children. These children also told Will, in front of his friends, that he was "a complete loser, and would never amount to anything in life."

Will was devastated, and broke down and cried at the insults, which only provoked further taunting. To make matters even worse, these bullies then rounded up the rest of Will's friends and asked them to play a game without Will, and the group ran off across the playground, leaving Will behind.

This situation continued for about a week before Will told me about it. This was not the first time Will had been bullied at school, but all the lessons about just walking away, or putting on a happy face and agreeing with what the other kids said, had been forgotten in the moment. So, we role played what Will could do and say when these kids attacked next. I encouraged him to go tell the playground monitor if things got really bad or if the kids used a lock-out strategy, where one child is barred from joining a game (something else these kids were up to).

We also talked at length about why kids do this type of thing to other kids. We talked about how these children were all new to the school and didn't have a lot of friends yet, how one split his time between several houses and nannies, and how another was much younger than his siblings and got very little supervision at home. Will came to realize that it wasn't him, but the other kids who had the problem, and that if they didn't tease Will, they'd be teasing other children (which in fact they were, as we found out later). This helped to depersonalize the situation and look at it from a more detached point of view.

Nevertheless, there will be times when you need to get involved directly. See Intervening When Things Get Bad later in this chapter.

Teaching Your Child to Be Selective of His Friends

One of the hardest lessons in this ordeal was to learn that a couple of kids who he thought were friends had turned on Will, and had joined up with the bullies. Will was then hit with the conflicted emotions of being hurt and wanting to be friends again with kids who had teased him. He made some social bids to try to patch things up, but they went afoul, and he realized that he had become the whipping boy instead of a peer. For example, they'd let him play Elimination with them if he agreed to always be the one to run and get the balls that bounced off into the field. He agreed for a day or two, wanting desperately to be part of this group, even though he knew he was being taken advantage of.

Over the period of a few days, we talked many times about Will's sense of self-worth, and how it was being jeopardized. He came to realize that he was worth more than this, and that no real friend would treat him this way. We role played standing up for himself by not agreeing to be the go-fer for lost balls, and he carried this out the next few days. The children did not let him play, so he left to go do something else. It was very painful to be excluded, but less painful than being taken advantage of by a few power-hungry kids. Will found other things to do with his time, and after several weeks, his true friends came back around.

Teaching Your Child to Take Care of Himself

When Will was in YMCA camp a few years ago, Pokémon cards were the rage. The counselors did not have a rule (at first) about bringing cards to camp, so many of the kids were bringing their cards in and trading them.

We had already had a bad experience with trading cards, where Will and some friends had traded cards, not really knowing their value. This led to all sorts of hard feelings when the children learned the value of the cards they had traded. Because I knew the parents involved, we were able to sort it all out, and we all talked to our children about fair trading and not taking advantage of other kids, especially those who did not know much about Pokémon cards and their relative worth.

In Y Camp, though, I didn't know the other kids, let alone their parents. For the first few days of camp, I was able to work with Will and make him understand that trading cards with these kids was a bad idea. But by the fourth day he came home telling me that one of the kids was willing to trade one of his holographic cards for one of Will's holographic cards. As Will had two of them, we agreed that it would be a fair trade, and I (foolishly) let him take the card to camp.

When I picked Will up that day, he was upset. I asked him what had happened, and he told me that he didn't get the card he wanted. I asked him what had transpired, and he reported that first he had traded the holographic card with the other kid as planned, but then his friend came up and offered Will two non-shiny cards for the holographic one. Will was torn, but the kids insisted that the two cards were worth more than the holographic card (which was retailing for $25 at local card stores). Will resisted until after lunch, when he agreed, finally, to trade his new holographic card. Later still, another kid came up and told Will that he would trade two of his cards for the two Will now had, plus he'd give him a nickel. Will didn't want to trade, but the three kids worked hard to convince him that it was a good deal. Under the pressure, Will finally relented and handed over the two cards to the third child. This kid then told Will that he only had one of the cards with him, and would bring the second card and the nickel the next day. He then handed Will a torn and bent card – and a very common one at that.

I felt awful, as I had let Will take this card to camp in the first place. What felt far worse, however, was the knowledge that these children knew that they could take advantage of Will and did so. Will and I had several conversations after this about taking care of yourself, and how, unfortunately, there are people in the world who aren't terribly nice, and will take advantage of you if given an opportunity.

It was a very hard lesson for Will, who is so trusting and open, like most children with AS. But it is a lesson all of these kids need, lest they become targets of predatory children.

Intervening When It Gets Bad

As a general rule, it's a good idea to let your child try to work out problematic situations on her own. But sometimes it doesn't work, and you'll need to intervene. For example, the bullying at school went on for so long (three weeks) and included so many other children (five targeted children that I knew of), that I felt that the school should get involved. I contacted the principal, who immediately called all the kids into his office, called the parents in, and stood guard on the playground to watch for any further incidents until the situation stabilized.

While I think it's a good idea to let your child work things out on his own with you scaffolding him at home, there are times when you simply have to get adults involved before irreparable damage is done. Where possible, work through the school and not with the other parents, so as to avoid bad blood between you and other families. If you know the parents well, you may want to talk to them in a nonjudgmental way about what is happening at school. Most parents are open to this type of information and will use it as their own teaching moments at home.

Make sure that part of your child's curriculum, either in the general classroom or in any social skills interventions he is receiving, includes how to handle bullies. This is absolutely key for AS kids. They need to be taught, repeatedly, how to handle bullies and predatory people in their lives. A very helpful book on bullying is *Perfect Targets: Asperger Syndrome and Bullying: Practical Solution for Surviving the Social World* by Rebekah Heinrichs (2002).

If bullying goes on at your school, and the school has been either unable or unwilling to foster a safe, kid-friendly environment, contact the school district. If that fails, you may want to take legal action to protect your child's rights. Bullying of any sort should not be tolerated, in theory or in practice, in the school environment. All children deserve a safe place to learn. Moreover, they have the legal right to a safe environment.

References

Heinrichs, R. (2002). *Perfect targets: Asperger Syndrome and bullying: Practical solution for surviving the social world*. Shawnee Mission, KS: Autism Asperger Publishing Company.

Chapter 9

Extracurricular Activities

Although your child's school day can provide much of her social interaction, you may need or want to look beyond the school experience for social contact for her. This is especially helpful if your child has been labeled as being odd or different by the other kids, and she is consistently being left out of peer activities. Sometimes, just getting out of her current social network is enough to foster a new friendship as it allows her to start over in a new situation.

Scouting

Scouts and related activities is great for many AS and NLD kids, as it provides a relatively structured environment in which to interact. Further, Girl Scouts, Cub Scouts, and Boy Scouts feature many areas in which your child may excel. Cub Scouts and Daisy and Brownie Girl Scouts have merit pins your child can acquire through work in chess, crafts, handmade games, and collections, as well as pins in community service, science, and the like. There is something for nearly every child.

Boy Scout troops often revolve around a specific focus, such as camping and orienteering, community service, and so forth. Junior and Cadet Girl Scout troops tend to be less topic-focused, but shopping around for a troop that your child might like is a good idea if there are several in your area.

Scouting in general fosters teamwork and may be good for your child. Be aware, however, that not all Scout troops are created equal. If the other kids (as well as parent leaders) are not good matches, it may be a painful experience, rather than a rewarding one.

Beyond Girl and Boy Scouts, there are other social groups such as Camp Fire Boys and Girls, 4-H, as well as other local outdoor groups. Check your phone book or the Internet for similar social experiences for your child.

Sports

Although most children with AS and NLD aren't crazy about sports, yours might be an exception and crave this type of activity. Additionally, all kids need physical activity and exposure to different sports, so I encourage you to get your child to participate in some sports in some way. Our rule at home is that Will has to be involved in at least one sport at a time to stay physically fit.

When your child is younger, I recommend going for the soccer, softball, baseball, and basketball teams, if at all possible. He may never be a star, and it may be hard for him to understand the rules and keep up, but some exposure to team sports is a good idea. Further, if you wait until the child is older, third grade and beyond, he is likely to feel very intimidated trying his hand at these games, even if he wants to, as several of his peers will by then be good at the game. It's better to start early when all of the kids are relatively new to the game.

But if your child doesn't get involved in sports early, don't give up entirely. New sports are introduced to kids as they move from elementary school to middle and high school. In our area, the "new" sports include tennis, swimming, volleyball, track and field, softball, and the biggie – football. In your area, you might also have lacrosse and hockey. When these sports are offered through the school, encourage your child to try out if she has any interest. While the other kids might be more athletic, few of the kids will have had prior experience in these sports, which tends to level the playing field a bit.

Like my son, your child will change and grow. In first grade, I pulled Will out of the local touch football league because he couldn't understand the game, was wildly frustrated, and cried in the middle of the field each game. It was painful for him, and for me. Now at 13, he jogs out to the field with the rest of the junior varsity team, and at 6', is a mighty presence. He is finally experiencing being part of a team.

Alternately, you can ask that your child "play down," which means that he is placed on a team with younger children. While he won't be playing with his peers, he will be playing with children who are closer to his ability range. Speak to the organizers or the coaches of the local team for more information about playing down. The downside is that he may be subjected to teasing by his peers, so make sure you give him some strategies about how to handle this, such as

"Hey, I'm just learning this game now, but watch out, and hope I'm on your team later!"

Another strategy that has worked for us is to try the less mainstream sports, such as football and roller hockey. While these sports are a bit rougher and more demanding, they are not as popular with school-age kids, so your child might be less intimidated to try them, and may be more successful with less competition from the hard-core jocks. He will likely be playing with kids he does not know yet (and who also are just learning). This is a good strategy for kids in fourth grade and above.

Kids with AS also do well in single or non-competitive sports, where they play against themselves or against a single opponent. These include track and field, skating, bowling, tennis, swimming, karate, and all the martial arts, orienteering, and gymnastics. All of these give your child the exercise she needs, teaches her the sportsmanship she should learn, and provides some social interaction.

You may be wondering whether or not to tell the coach or instructor that your child has special needs prior to starting a season. I can't tell you what to do here. You need to play it by ear. On the one hand, the ultimate goal is to ensure that your child is treated like every other child, able to join in, learn the game, cope with frustration, and shine with enthusiasm when she succeeds. On the other hand, some children have a truly difficult time just hanging in, and if the coach thinks her behavior stems from stubbornness or willfulness, your child may be reprimanded unnecessarily.

View your child in comparison to the other children, and watch how the coach interacts with her. If you sense that there may be trouble, or that your child is really struggling, take the coach aside and inform him that your child has a learning disorder and has difficulty in adapting to team sports. Then, work with the coach as you can to accommodate – for the team's and your child's benefits. This may mean that instead of playing a whole period, she only plays half, or that the coach gives her subtle cues to pay attention to the game instead of drifting off.

As with Scouting, you may run across a parent whose tolerance and/or abilities are tested by your child. If things don't work out and it's truly painful for your child to remain in the sport, remove her from the team. It's better to leave than to reinforce in your child that team sports are painful.

Clubs

Clubs are another way to get your child involved socially or physically. Depending on where you live and what type of activities you and your child like, you could investigate 4-H clubs, swimming clubs, chess clubs, and so on.

Many school districts have after-school clubs for upper-elementary and junior high and high school students, which can be a real boon for AS kids who don't have many friends and little to do besides play Nintendo. Getting your child involved in photography, computer programming, web design, computer animation, horticulture, or astronomy might not only be a great new diversion and social opportunity, it could turn into a career. Additionally, academic clubs for math and science might be just the ticket.

Encourage your child to try different activities, even if you suspect that they may not pan out. You might be wrong, and your child may find something compelling to involve himself with. And even if you're right and he drops it after a semester, he will have tried something new and broadened his horizons a bit.

Church, Synagogue, Temple, or Mosque

If your family follows a particular faith, attending church, synagogue, temple, or mosque youth groups can be a great way to get your child involved with other children. First off, most groups revolving around a faith organization are tolerant and forgiving, and your child may find a welcome home where he is accepted for who he is.

Additionally, many faith youth groups do community or social outreach work, which is a great way to teach your child about empathy and reciprocity and aiding those less fortunate than ourselves. This is a lesson all children need, but the self-focused AS kid needs in extra doses.

Even if your family does not regularly attend faith services, you may be able to find an organization that meets your beliefs and that can benefit your child. Many churches have become functionally non-denominational: The Unitarian-Universalist Church, for example, welcomes people of all faiths – as well as atheists and agnostics – with a strong focus on community outreach and social justice.

Camps

We've already talked about having themed summer or break camps in your backyard, but if that's too much for you, there are plenty of wonderful programs in most areas that will suit your child. Depending on where you live, you might find oceanography camps, tennis camps, swim camps, computer camps, and so forth. Work with your child to determine what he might be interested in, and then scout around either in local parenting magazines or on the Internet (see Resources & References for more information).

Even if you can't find a camp that meets your child's interests locally, you might be able to combine a family vacation around a themed camp. Four years ago, we went to San Diego for a week so that Will could attend a camp offered by Scripps Oceanographic Society. I got a hotel room and lounged on the beach while he was in camp, and in the afternoons and evenings we went to all of the local attractions, such as the San Diego Zoo.

If your child cannot handle a full program without an aide or intervention, you can do one of two things. First, if there is a camp your child would really like to attend, contact the organization and see if they can make accommodations for your child. Explain what his needs are likely to be. If the organization is willing to step up, it might be worth trying, even if you have to abort the experiment part-way through. The second thing you can try is to locate camps that focus on accommodating kids who may not be successful in a regular day camp. Once your child gets the hang of camp, he may be willing (and able) to be mainstreamed into a regular camp.

Vacations

There are two types of vacations: totally "vegged-out" vacations where you do nothing but relax and vacations where you are out to do or see something. And, of course, there are vacations that combine both elements.

With an AS or NLD kid, you might go nuts on a relaxing vacation because there is not enough to do, and because these kids are notoriously short on self-entertaining skills (other than GameBoy). You might as well have stayed at home. On the other hand, you might have a kid who so loves the water that a trip to a Hawaiian island might be heaven on earth. Only you will know.

The most important thing to do before planning a vacation is to honestly assess the personality types in your family and see which kind of vacation fits. The way to have a miserable vacation is to force a sightseeing trip on a family who would rather play in the pool, or to try to get some rest and relaxation with a group of kids who need to be entertained 24/7. Often compromises can be made, where you can do a little of both types in a single vacation, if that's what the family's composite personality dictates.

If your family is going to take a "doing" vacation, you may want to look into vacation spots that play off your children's interests. For example, if you have a dinosaur freak in your midst, consider going to Colorado, Wyoming, Utah, or Montana where there are plenty of dig sites you can visit to get your complete prehistoric fill. Pokémon is his love? See if you can get a tour of the NamePhreak company in Seattle. If sea creatures are his cup of tea, maybe the Florida Keys are a good bet for you and yours.

Think creatively about what your child (or children) like, and see if you can come up with a vacation that works for everyone – a little quiet time for mom and dad, fun sights for the kids, and so on. These types of vacations build lifetime memories, and are sure to involve your child more fully in the "vacation" moment.

As you are planning your trip, don't forget to think through any special travel needs your child might have. Does he have a wheat allergy? Make sure you take non-wheat snacks and breads on the trip. Need to have some quiet time every few hours? Don't book an 8-hour flight; take a stopover midway through the trip. Think ahead so that the trip is rewarding for everyone.

Hobbies

Whatever happened to hobbies? I remember well the hours that my older brother put into his coin collection and building of model cars. He'd spend days on these pastimes, sometimes alone and sometimes with a friend or two. In an age of instant gratification, hobbies seem to be a thing of the past. Or are they?

For a kid with AS who likes to sort things, catalog things, and memorize things, a collecting hobby could be ideal. Further, for kids who need some help in fine-motor skills, building replicas (starting with easier kits) could build these skills – as well as patience.

If your child hasn't been exposed to a good old-fashioned hobby, maybe a trip down to the local stamp collecting shop or hobby shop would be worthwhile. Additionally, there are often social clubs associated with hobbies that your child might find appealing, or maybe you have an older relative or friend with a unique hobby she might want to share with your child. This is a great way for your AS child to connect with the world outside. And as mentioned earlier, hobbies and special interests can sometimes be parlayed into a future career.

Chapter 10

Nervous Habits and Warning Signs

One of the sure-fire ways your child will fail socially is if she has an obvious, outward manifestation of her condition that others find discomfiting. Some of these behaviors are harmless in themselves, but others may be signs of deeper issues. If your child displays any of these outward habits or symptoms of her disorder, read this chapter to learn what can be done to help address or modify them so your child can be successful.

Nervous Habits

Some of the hallmarks of children who fall within the autism spectrum are motor irregularities or obsessive-compulsive behaviors. These can be mild and only appear when a child is very excited or upset, or they may be aggravated and happen nearly continuously. Although harmless in themselves, they call attention to the child in ways that make him stand out as being different, and all but the most tolerant children tend to avoid kids who manifest these symptoms.

The behaviors described here are soothing or stimulating to the child, and you should be mindful of this whenever planning or implementing an intervention to modify or change them. Yelling, name calling, and shaming are definite no-nos when addressing these issues, and will severely undermine the child's self-esteem. It is critical that other adults and children aren't allowed to use these detrimental tactics either.

Additionally, repeatedly calling attention to the behaviors and simply telling the child to stop is also not likely to work. Generally speaking, in order to "extinguish" a behavior that causes immediate relief from stress, a replacement behavior that satisfies that same need but in a more socially acceptable way must be introduced.

I worked with one local AS expert who felt that the secondary "relief" behavior should be used as a reward after a child has not displayed the original, disruptive behavior for a period of time. I disagreed then, and I disagree now, as her intervention goes against both common sense and most cognitive-behavior therapy (CBT) techniques used to control anxiety (http://www.jabramowitz.com/CBT.html). Look to someone who is undergoing smoking cessation. Is he going to stay away from cigarettes all day if he knows he will get a whole bag of carrots at 5:00? No. While the person is learning new and more adaptive ways to cope with anxiety, especially for people who crave sensory input, an immediate but healthier substitute may be in order.

What you can do to praise your child's efforts is to offer irregular rewards after a set period of time when the secondary behavior is consistently used. But these rewards should not take the place of the outlet (the secondary behavior) the child needs to calm and/or stimulate himself.

Hand Flapping

Hand flapping is a classic autistic symptom, and one of the harder ones to curb. When a child is little, it isn't terribly disruptive, but as the child reaches the upper-elementary grades, he begins to stand out if hand flapping manifests frequently. This behavior tends to happen more often when the child is in an unstructured setting, such as on the playground waiting for his turn at bat, where he might concurrently be trying to control his anxiety and his excitement and summon his patience.

Start by asking the child how he feels when he flaps his hands – is he nervous, excited, scared? This may take a few tries, and your own observation will help a great deal in pinpointing when the behavior occurs and what is happening in the child's body at the time.

After determining what the primary cause (or causes) for the behavior is, you can introduce an alternative. If he is excited, for example, ask him if he can clap or jump up and down instead (clapping for a teammate up at bat is a little more "socially acceptable" than flapping your hands). This will probably give him the stimulus he needs to keep his body in check. You can also model this behavior for him, encouraging him to clap when things get exciting.

If he is hand flapping because of anxiety, try keeping a Koosh ball or some other small fidget in his pocket (or one in each pocket), and redirect him to that item when he is nervous. You can use a keyword such as "Pockets!" when he begins to flap his hands due to anxiety. Rubbing his back and speaking soothingly usually also helps lower anxiety.

With both of these examples, your child may learn these new secondary behaviors in your presence but have a hard time generalizing the behavior at school or when you are not around. This inability to generalize a behavior to different situations is very common. Speak to your child's teachers and coaches, and tell them what you are doing so that they can help reinforce these new behaviors when you are absent.

In the meantime, don't give up at home. Keep up the reminders, and eventually your child will become so used to the secondary behavior that the first will likely diminish.

Rocking

Like hand flapping, rocking is a common symptom of an autism spectrum disorder. It differs from hands flapping in that it can be clearly linked to the child's need for sensory input to calm herself, specifically for what are known as vestibular and proprioceptive motions (*vestibular* refers to balance and *proprioceptive* refers to the tension felt in the muscles and tendons during movement). However, like hand flapping, rocking tends to manifest when a child is excited or nervous.

Start by identifying what types of situations tend to provoke this behavior so that you can be more alert to your child's sensitivities. The replacement behaviors that work best for rocking are those that give your child's body what it is craving – specific types of movement – in order to stay alert or to calm down. These include swinging, jumping on a trampoline, lifting or pushing heavy items, rocking in a rocking chair, and so on.

Obviously, none of these options works terribly well in a classroom. If your child has a hard time sitting still and constantly rocks back and forth to get her body where it needs to be, you can ask for a proprioceptive mat for her to sit on (an air-filled mat that gives the body some of the motion that it craves) or have her sit on a giant ball (called a therapy ball) or a T-Stool (one-legged stool) to sit on. All of these are items commonly used in occupational therapy, and if your school does not have them or will not purchase them for your child, you may consider buying them yourself – you can find them on the Internet. See also the Resources & References section for more information.

At recess time, make sure your child is out on the swings or jumping, and maybe even carrying heavy boxes for her teacher so that she gets the physical activity she craves.

Fidgeting

Although I don't have Asperger Syndrome, I am a first-class fidgeter. Fidgeting for me is an organizing behavior that helps me focus on what I am listening to or doing. I fidget when I'm in class, when I'm in meetings, when I'm watching TV, and so forth. When I was little, I twirled my hair. In grade school, I chewed pencils. When I was old enough to start wearing jewelry, I began to fidget with my rings. I still do it at age 48!

Fidgeting is a relatively "normal" activity, up until it becomes distracting to others, just like rocking and hand flapping (there's absolutely nothing wrong with these activities in and of themselves). So, if your child is a fidgeter, the first thing to assess is how distracting the fidgeting is to those around him. If it is a problem, then an intervention may be in order. If it seems to annoy only you, maybe biting your tongue is more reasonable.

If you've decided that the behavior is disruptive, remember that it is your child's unconscious way of getting her body to "behave" in a stressful or exciting situation. As with hand flapping, giving your child a focused secondary behavior to occupy her hands is likely to do the trick. This could be a Koosh ball, another type of squeeze ball, Wikki Stix, and so on, for her to play with at her desk or in her pocket. If this is seen as too disruptive for the classroom (some teachers have very low thresholds for fidgeting), you could stick a piece of adhesive-backed Velcro on the underside of her desk or on the inside of her binder, for her to fidget with. You could also thread three or four buttons on a piece of string and let her manipulate those under the desk with her free hand. Quietly, of course!

As with the hand flapping, try one of these interventions at home first to reinforce the behavior in a relatively non-stressful setting. Once the child gets the hang of it, talk to her teacher, and have her use it at school.

Nose Picking and Other Annoyances

The school-age debate rages among children as to who picks their noses and who doesn't, but the truth of the matter is, it's pretty disgusting, and no kid wants to hang with a child who does it on a regular basis. The same goes for scab picking, ear tugging, pencil tapping, and so forth. These behaviors tend to drive others wild, and are best handled early on and as gently, but forcefully, as possible.

Intervene with these behaviors just like you would with the others listed above: Find out what situations make the child crave the stimulation; find an appropriate secondary behavior; start intervention at home; and work on generalizing it to the school setting with the teacher's help. Your child will be more "integratable" if he can lose these habits.

A Quick-Pick List of Sensory Stimuli

Sensory integration will likely be a big part of your strategy to help your AS child. Many, if not most, of these kids need help with "self-regulating" their bodies to stay alert and calm, and there are many excellent resources available to parents to learn how to work with your child in this area.

Some of the best books on the subject are *The Out-of-Sync Child* by Carol Kranowitz (2006) and *Asperger Syndrome and Sensory Issues* by Brenda Myles and colleagues (2000). You can also find several websites devoted to sensory integration and therapeutic interventions. For children with severe sensory deficits and maladaptive behaviors, you may want to try a psychological intervention such as cognitive behavior therapy (CBT). Refer to the Resources & References chapter for more information. In the meantime, the following table gives you some ideas of what types of stimuli you can try for different types of disruptive behaviors.

Behavior	What the Body Is Saying	Possible Interventions
Touches everything and everyone	*I need stimulus!*	When possible, let your child explore his world with his hands.
		Give your child tactile toys to play with during his free time.
		Give your child fidgets to keep his hands where they "belong."
		If during floor activity, mark a boundary on the floor with tape.
		If during floor activity, give the child a pillow to squeeze.
		If during lineup, let the child be first in line or mark a standing place on the ground with tape.
		Work on social skills around touching, personal space, and physical safety.

Behavior	What the Body Is Saying	Possible Interventions
Slumps in chair	*I can't stay alert!*	Allow child to stand during activity.
		Have child sit on proprioceptive mat/therapy ball/T-stool.
		Have child push or pull heavy items during recess.
		Give frequent movement breaks.
		Put tennis balls on two opposite legs of chairs to give slight movement.
Chews on pencils, pens, straws	*I need calming or organizing!*	Allow child to chew on coffee stirrer or straw.
		Place 3-inch length of latex tubing on end of pencil for child to chew on.
		Give child celery, crackers, gummy worms, hard candy as snacks.
		Give child water bottle with strong straw.
Hates washing face, combing hair	*I hate being touched there!*	Desensitize by lightly rubbing around mouth area with dry washcloth.
		Desensitize by stroking head with firm hand.
		Use firmer pressure.
		Cut hair short.
		Let child wash face and comb hair.

Behavior	What the Body Is Saying	Possible Interventions
Talks/hums constantly	*I need organizing!*	Allow the child to talk or hum if it does not bother anyone.
		Teach the child to talk or hum more quietly.
		Block out other noises that may be interfering with concentration.
		If humming, give child an electric toothbrush at home for vibration sensation.
		If talking, give child a fidget to play with at desk.
Doesn't like certain clothes	*I hate the way this feels!*	Buy clothes that don't bother your child.
		Desensitize by rubbing child's body with towel.
		Remove tags.
		Use fragrance-free, non-irritating detergents.
		Rinse clothes twice after washing.

Fearful Behavior

Some, but not all, children with AS have what seem to be un-reasonable fears or phobias that can interfere with their daily lives. I've seen children who were afraid of grass, afraid of people in uniform, and afraid of stuffed animals. While all young children can be fearful of one thing or another, many children with AS have this type of fearful behavior longer and more intensely, and tend to be fearful of unusual things.

On occasion, these fears can lead to out-and-out phobias or contribute to obsessive-compulsive behaviors.

When Will was very, very young, he was fearful of ghosts – pictures of them, cartoons of them, and especially Halloween decorations that depicted them. The most amazing part of this fear was that it manifested in Will when he was less than a year old. To this day, I don't know why or how he could have developed a fear of something he had no "spooky" associations with.

Every year at Halloween, we had a hard time keeping images of ghosts from him. He was frightened of ghost decorations and spooky ghost sounds, and refused to watch any movies or TV shows with ghosts in them. There were even certain songs that he couldn't listen to because the singing reminded him of ghosts. I tried some desensitization with him, but to no avail. Every time I even mentioned a ghost, he became panicky. Luckily, he grew out of it at around age 11.

When he was about 7, he went on a field trip to a natural science museum. I was a group leader, and we had finished the exhibit a bit early, so we walked through a special exhibit on germs. It was very cool, with brightly colored "germs" decorating the walls, and exhibits on "germs through the ages" showed displays of how our ancestors discovered germs, how they learned to sterilize items, and so forth. There were a couple of tastefully done dioramas of the Black Plague and other major catastrophes, but nothing that was terribly frightening or alarming.

Will became absolutely panic-stricken about 10 minutes into the visit. The other four boys in our group were excited about looking at germs through a microscope, and learning about good germs and bad germs, but Will was becoming physically distressed, pulling on his jacket, fidgeting, and wringing his hands. Eventually, we all had to leave the exhibit. For five months afterward, Will remained in an absolute fear of germs, washing his hands several times a day, refusing to touch food that had been handled by someone other than me, and so on. He asked a hundred questions about germs – Will they get me in my bed? What happens if a germ flies in my mouth? What if the cat touches my toothbrush while I'm at school? Suddenly, as quickly as the fear came, it went, but it was miserable living through this.

Will also had a panic attack over a dummied-up picture of a murder scene in a science camp. After I spoke to him about this, it became clear that he was unable to distinguish between reality and fiction, and thought not only that the murder victim in the picture was real, but that the picture itself was real. This inability to distinguish real from representation from fiction seems to be the root of the other fears as well. Real ghosts (if there are such things) would be scary to many of us, but not their representations. Germs are real and some can hurt us, but the germs in the exhibit were not real – yet Will panicked anyway, and then let that cause him to panic over an extended time about these "unseen" germs which were, he believed, everywhere, ready to attack.

If your AS child is overly fearful about an item or topic, try to understand if it is a representational issue, such as Will's seemed to be. If so, work on distinguishing between what is real, representation, and fiction. If his fears don't abate in a reasonable time, consult a professional for help.

Rude Behavior

One of the most devastating aspects of the behavior of kids with AS is that while they are frequently very sweet and kind (once you get to know them), they are often rude, bossy, and inflexible in their interactions. If taken to the extreme, these behaviors will cause all sorts of problems for your child, from getting in repeated trouble with his teachers, to a continued inability to make friends. And, for better or worse, you as a parent will often be called to task for your child's "monstrous" behavior, and you will likely be the subject of nasty looks and comments, as well as well-meaning, if totally useless, advice.

In order for your child to grow into a well-functioning adult, you have to work with her at an early age to help her learn better interaction tools.

Imperious Behavior

When Will was in second grade, his peers repeatedly called him a show-off because he talked endlessly, and authoritatively, on any subject he knew something about. These "conversations" were nearly always one-sided: a veritable litany of encyclopedic facts. Further, he had no patience for children who didn't know as much as he did, rolling his eyes or sighing deeply when someone mispronounced a dinosaur's name, for example. He also could not contain himself when playing Nintendo or any other game he had mastered, and would repeatedly yank the controls from his friend to "show him how to do it." Needless to say, these were all very disastrous behaviors in terms of developing peer relationships.

At the heart of this imperious behavior is the AS child's inability to understand how another person feels at a given time. It never occurred to Will that any of these actions had a deleterious effect on social interactions, and he was befuddled when his friends stomped off in a huff.

He just didn't get it. And so, he had to be taught directly. If at all possible, get help from your child's speech and language professional, but also work on this at home. It is not a good idea to simply hope she grows out of this phase, because she won't, and if there is anything worse than an imperious child, it's an imperious adult.

Interventions that are typically used for this type of behavior are of the role-playing type. Probably the best known examples are *Carol Gray's Social Stories™*, which describe a variety of social situations and ask the child to work through what responses are appropriate and why. Gray's books instruct parents and teachers on how to write a custom Social Story™ for the child, and are very useful resources that you can turn to time and time again. Two of Gray's newer books, *The New Social Story™ Book* (2000) and *My Social Stories™ Book* (2002) are particularly good.

You can create a similar type of tool by writing or typing up situations that you know your child has trouble in. Then work through the whats and whys of appropriate responses with him. Do the same story each day for a week to ensure that the message is reinforced.

Once mastered, have your child try to generalize the message into everyday life. For example, if he has had problems not yanking a GameBoy from his sister when she kills the wrong alien, you might follow a pattern like this:

1) Create your homemade story; for example:
   Jimmy likes to play GameBoy, and so does his sister Susan. Jimmy gets frustrated when Susan makes a mistake at GameBoy and wants to take the game away from her to do it right. This makes Susan sad and mad. Jimmy will try to be patient with her, and let her play the game the way she knows how.

2) Read this story together with your child every day at a quiet time. Talk about what it would feel like if a GameBoy was yanked away from him. Would it make him feel sad, bad, what?

3) Observe his behavior at home with Susan. Praise him when he keeps his cool, give him gentle reminders when he goes after the GameBoy (Jimmy, remember our story?).

4) Once he has mastered this (or nearly so), ask him what other situations he can apply his patience to at school and at home. Ask him to try one new situation to see if he can generalize this new skill.

5) Follow up with him on how he is doing. If he is struggling to generalize this skill to another situation, create a new story for that particular issue. Some kids have a difficult time applying an abstract concept to real life.

As repetitive as this may seem, it works. Repetition is the key, as these kids are often not able to learn social skills intuitively the way the rest of us do. Keep your wits, your patience, and your sense of humor, and you'll work through it all.

Yakety-Yak

Along with imperious behavior, incessant or one-way talking is a sure-fire way to lose friends. Conversations are wonderful conglomerates of social interaction skills – verbal and nonverbal messages are sent, received, integrated, and acted upon without any thought. For most of us, that is.

For a kid with AS, however, conversations can be baffling. There are times when you are supposed to maintain eye gaze, and times when you are supposed to look away. There are times when you are supposed to smile, frown, look astonished, or look serious when listening. You are supposed to learn how and when to interject a comment or question without breaking the flow of conversation. You are supposed to keep your thoughts on this topic, and then learn how to change the subject to something else – without hurting the other person's feelings.

You are supposed to learn how to ask relevant questions, how to offer supporting looks, gestures, and words. In short, you are supposed to be able to mind-read what the other person is thinking and feeling, so that you can act accordingly. Talk about hard!

The best way to teach your child appropriate conversational skills is through practice, both structured and unstructured. Your child will get some guidance (though not enough) in the general education classroom along with the other children (nearly every young child has a hard time learning not to interrupt, for example). Additionally, she should receive specific pragmatic speech interventions to learn how to carry on a two-way conversation: how to listen, maintain eye gaze, ask appropriate questions (remain on topic), how to change subjects (and when), and so on.

Work should also be done on reading other people's non-verbal cues, such as facial expressions and body language. You can do this at home as well, by making faces and having your child guess what expression you are making. Focus should also be given to his own body language and facial expression by directly teaching him, using a mirror, how to "look surprised" or "look happy." This will go a long way in helping him.

Again, you can use Social Stories™ for situations that are pervasive, such as interrupting in class or staying on topic. You can also use behavior modification techniques by putting eye contact on cue. This is done by telling your child that every time you use his name (or touch him on the shoulder, if he responds more to physical touch), he is to look at you.

At first, he likely won't look at you, so gently lift his chin up and remind him that every time you use his name, you'd like him to look at you. After a while, he will look up, and after he has mastered that, you can have him maintain eye gaze for a few seconds, building up to longer periods. Then, generalize this approach to the classroom and social interactions with adults who can also put him on cue.

At home, you can also work on not interrupting, staying on topic, and gently leading him away from monologues, where he recites facts rather than engaging in a true conversation.

> *"What did you do at school today, Will?"*
>
> *"Not much; we had a test before recess and then I played with Greg."*
>
> *"Cool. How do you think you did on the test? Did the studying help, do you think?"*
>
> *"I don't know. Can Greg come over today? We want to keep working on the Pokémon list we started."* *(Does not remain on topic.)*
>
> *"Well, maybe later. Can you tell me more about the test? I'm really curious."*
>
> *"Charizard and Charmander both have fewer hit points than Mewto, but in my GameBoy, Mewto always loses in a battle against them. We want to find out what other Pokémon this works for."* *(Ignores redirect, changes topic again inappropriately.)*

"Will, right now I'm not interested in Pokémon."

"I think it might also happen for Bulbasaur ..."

"Sweetie, right now I don't want to hear any more about Pokémon. I'm not very interested in Pokémon. What does my face tell you? Does my face tell you that I'm interested in what you are saying?"

While this off-topic behavior might be age-appropriate for a younger child, it is not appropriate for a 10-year-old. This doesn't mean that you should cut your child off whenever he talks about a subject he is interested in, but you should intervene when he is repeatedly off topic. Draw his attention to the fact, gently, that he is not answering your questions, that he is not reading your cues, and that he has to engage in a conversation with you. This may take years of work. Hang in and be patient. He will show improvement as time goes by.

Teaching conversation skills is very, very complex, and you probably need professional interventions in this area if your child is to be successful. This doesn't mean you can't work on this at home (you should), but what I've described here are very high-level tasks you can use to help him. Insist on getting him qualified intervention at school, and if that doesn't work, locate a speech pathologist who works with autistic spectrum kids and pay for the services yourself. This intervention is a must-have.

Rigidity and Inflexibility

Many AS kids depend on rote schedules and behaviors to get them through the day. A schedule gives them comfort in a confusing world – the less they have to work through on the fly, the better they seem to function.

While putting a schedule in place is relatively easy, there are many areas when a schedule is not possible, or times when a child needs to deviate from a schedule. This can lead to chaos and upset on the part of the child, and for that reason, it's a good idea to try to imbue your child with a sense of flexibility.

Ironically, I have found that the best way to increase flexibility is to first have a set schedule that the child can rely on. Because schedules are comforting, it's easier to move to a new behavior (increased flexibility) when the child is comfortable and relaxed, rather than when she is nervous and anxious (which is often caused by a lack of a schedule).

In school and at home, have a chart that describes what happens every day (or most days). For pre-readers or kids who are more visually oriented, you can use pictures from magazines instead of words. Include on your child's chart the following items:

In the Morning:

- ❐ Get up

- ❐ Brush teeth

- ❐ Get dressed

- ❐ Eat breakfast

- ❐ Gather school materials

- ❐ Get lunch

- ❐ Say goodbye

- ❐ Smile

In the Afternoon:

- ❏ Put lunch box in kitchen

- ❏ Get snack

- ❏ Do homework

- ❏ Put homework in binder

- ❏ Help set table

In the Evening:

- ❏ Take bath

- ❏ Brush teeth

- ❏ Put on PJs

- ❏ Get clothes out for tomorrow

Modify this, as needed, for your child, and post the chart somewhere where he will see it every day. For the classroom, have the teacher create a similar chart for your child, noting all regular activities such as recess, lunch, reading time, homework check-in, science, and so forth. As a child gets older, it's very useful to have a checklist in his binder indicating all of the "usual things" he needs to collect before going home.

Once your child is comfortable with this schedule and can depend on it to get through her day (depending on your child, this may take quite some time, or happen very quickly), you can begin to interject some flexibility in the routine. Whenever your child's routine changes, either because you want to build flexibility or because something interrupts the usual schedule, make sure to give your child plenty of advance notice. Also instruct her teacher to do the same.

- ❏ "Tomorrow we have to go to the dentist right after school. I'll bring a snack in the car, and you'll do your homework when we get done, okay?"

- ❏ "Next week we won't be having science in the afternoon because the class will be taking the STAR test all week. Also, recess will be 15 minutes earlier than normal."

- ❏ "We'll have to skip your bath on Saturday because we'll be at Gramma's house."

All of these messages alert your child that something will be different, and she can start working through how she needs to react to these changes well in advance. Most children learn flexibility naturally and can shift seamlessly between a schedule and deviations from the schedule without too much trouble. Children with AS need to be taught how to process these changes, however.

Once your child becomes more comfortable with small deviations from the schedule, you can introduce more changes – dinner after bathtime, homework after dinner, and so on, until one day when you may be able to drop all formal schedules.

You can use this approach on nearly any rote behavior your child demonstrates by following the same formula: establish a pattern or schedule and acknowledge that it gives comfort to your child. Without abandoning the pattern completely, slowly introduce changes to the pattern. As the child incorporates this disruption to the pattern, you can add more disruption.

During times of stress, your child will likely regress to the rote pattern or schedule. Let him. He finds comfort in it, and forcing a child to be flexible when he is fearful only reinforces the need for the schedule or pattern. This is common and useful human behavior, and must be treated with sensitivity.

Inappropriate Behavior

Like any child, kids with AS display inappropriate behavior from time to time. The difference is (or may be) that the child is not fully aware that his behavior is inappropriate, or if he is, he may not understand the extent to which it is inappropriate.

For example, a child may have a vague understanding that it's not okay to stick his hands in his pants during recess, but he doesn't understand that it is a social taboo to play with one's genitals in public in the second grade. Unable to read the look of shock and horror on people's faces, he may simply be pleased that anyone is responding to him at all in a social context.

Quickly intervene as described under Imperious Behavior, and make sure he begins to learn that this type of behavior is upsetting to those around him, and is not okay. If the behavior seems to stem from anxiety, consider implementing a fidget for him as described in the section Quick-Pick List of Sensory Stimuli.

Do these interventions quickly and with the help of his teachers at school. Nothing does more lasting harm to a child socially than picking up a truly inappropriate behavior and then demonstrating it in front of his peers. While the behavior may only last a week or two, your child's peers will remember it for years to come. Immediate intervention is key.

A behavior that Will picked up is a very good example. In second grade, several boys taunted Will, encouraging him to kiss a girl in class while he was waiting in line. Because Will was so starved for social interaction (and because he didn't realize how "wrong" this was), he did it – to the delight of the other boys, and the horror of the little girl. This went on for a week before I heard about it. Will told me that the kids at school had named him "Kissy Boy," and I was dismayed when I learned why.

After telling Will firmly but kindly that this behavior had to stop right away, I went to his teacher, his principal, and his speech teacher. The teacher and speech pathologist both were aware that Will was being called "Kissy Boy," but had done nothing to find out why. I came unglued! I asked them to intervene immediately, and watch the children on the playground to make sure that the egging on stopped. I also asked the teacher to move Will away from the kids who were doing this, and from the three girls he had kissed.

After a week when I learned that nothing had been done, and that Will was still being harassed every single day, I told the school officials that if I, as Will's mother, was sued for sexual harassment, I would in turn sue the district for not intervening to stop this situation as it was out of my control.

The school finally intervened, but four years later children in Will's class still remembered when he was Kissy Boy and occasionally teased him about it. Please don't give in to your desire to "cute-ify" this type of behavior, or ignore it in any way. You must intervene if your child gets caught up in a behavior that is inappropriate. If you don't, your child will suffer the consequences for years to come.

Acting-Out Behavior

Acting out is similar to inappropriate behavior. Acting out may manifest as aggression against others, aggression against self, or tantrums. But the stakes are higher because your child could become a threat to himself or to someone else.

Acting out is appropriately named in that it generally appears when a child is "acting out" his or her inner feelings – often of frustration, fear, or depression. This is key to remember, because it is easy to view this type of behavior as willful or malicious. It is not.

Aggressive Behavior

Aggressive behavior may present in younger children as biting, kicking, scratching, or hitting. In older children, it usually presents itself as hitting or pushing. As with so many other facets of the behaviors of an AS child, the key to stopping this behavior for good is to understand its motive.

Children usually act aggressively when they feel threatened, just like adults do. Children have very little control over their daily lives – the adults in their worlds decide where they will live, what they will eat for lunch, maybe what they wear, sometimes who their friends are. Such lack of control can be frustrating to all kids, and to heap AS on top of it adds fuel to the fire. These kids can't seem to control the social world around them like other kids, can't seem to control how they act in front of their peers, can't seem to get a hold on their schoolwork, and so on. It's a lot to bear.

So, while absolutely unacceptable, it's not a great surprise that when someone calls a child with AS a geek to his face for the fifth time that week, and in front of his friends, the kid may lose it and haul off and smack the other child. These kids are often so short on coping skills, it's a wonder it doesn't happen more often given the torment they often face.

If this happens to your child, or if she is biting or kicking or hitting, immediately speak to the school staff about what is happening in school. Has there been an increase in class work? Is your child sitting next to someone who is bothering her? Does she seem to be slipping in her academic work? Also, don't forget to look at home. Did Mom just go back to work? Is there a new sibling on the way? Is Dad traveling a lot for business?

Be aware that many school districts may label your child as simply lacking impulse control if she is aggressive toward others, and while this is true up to a point, you need to make it clear to them that she would not act this way without being provoked or triggered in some fashion. This is not to minimize the seriousness of the offense, but if the school staff uses only punishment to rectify the situation, they have missed the mark and proven by their actions that they do not understand Asperger Syndrome.

Aggression often indicates that a child feels out of control or that his world is out of control. Because children with AS tend to be the antithesis of your classic sociopath (who acts out due to lack of regard for others), there is nearly always a discernible trigger.

When Will was in preschool, he had a terrible biting problem. This went on for almost 18 months, causing a great deal of disruption in his classroom (and was the reason why we took him in for psychological testing in the first place). The staff was very savvy, and knew that simple punishment was not going to work. Instead, they removed him from the room after biting, had him apologize when he cooled off a little later, showed him the "wound" he had caused on the other child, and told him that he had to use his words when he got upset.

He was closely observed by the staff, and each time he looked as if he was going to lose it and take a bite out of a child, they would jump in and tell him, "Use your words." Eventually, the biting stopped. Punishment alone, without understanding that the biting mechanism was a nonverbal "get out of my space, you're intruding" message, would not have helped Will at all. He needed help to learn how to interact because he couldn't figure it out on his own.

Since starting elementary school, Will has gotten into three "fights" with other children, where he hit or punched another kid. While I do not condone his actions, a little research showed that each time he was teased by the person who got hit. The teaching moment, then, is to instruct your child to walk away when someone teases or provokes him. While it is wrong to tease someone, it is equally wrong to hit.

If you face a situation like this, make sure you communicate to the school staff what discipline you are using at home (there should be some consequence to strongly make the point), and what message you have given your child about physical force. You should also tell the staff that your child was provoked, and how he was provoked, and assertively remind them that he should be safe from all bullying at his school.

A Word of Warning

If the school staff uses terms such as "oppositional" or "defiant" when talking about your child and his behavior, quickly intervene on his behalf. These words are used for children whose behaviors are consciously manipulative and do not apply to a child who has Asperger Syndrome. If you cannot convince the school that your child is not behaving in a defiant manner, seriously consider hiring an educational advocate. The course of interventions the school may use for dealing with a defiant child will not work and may, in fact, be emotionally damaging to your AS kid.

Destructive Behavior

Truly destructive behavior, including destroying property, is rare in children with AS. These kids tend to be naïve, and generally don't have the social prowess to destroy property out of vengeance, pleasure, or disobedience. They lack all of these talents, thankfully.

Having said that, if your child is caught destroying property, either defacing school walls, stealing a kid's lunch, or ripping up his sister's clothes, look at what is happening in his life that is causing him to behave this way. It could be that he is furious with all of the attention his sister is getting for going on a special trip for school, or that he stole a kid's lunch because someone stole his, or that someone egged him on to take a marker to the janitor's door. This does not mean that he should not be held accountable, it just means that there is likely to be a trigger somewhere for these behaviors. Find the trigger, and you can begin to address the underlying problem, and devise a plan.

If your child manifests destructive behaviors over a period of time and you are unable to identify a reason for the behavior, I strongly recommend that you get a referral to a psychiatrist to find out what is troubling your child.

Tantrums

Ah, tantrums. What parent's life would be complete without them? And while your friends' children outgrow tantrums by, say, age 6 or 7, yours may continue for a while longer. And if they do continue much beyond this "normal" age range, remember that he may be breaking the unwritten rules of "big boys don't cry," and may be teased for his "babyish" behavior. Don't let tantrums go unchecked. Find out what is triggering them.

Just as with other kids, start with the basics. Is your child hungry? Tired? Bored? Frustrated? Cold? Take care of her basic needs first, and remember that while other children learn to ask for help with these needs ("Mom, I'm starved!"), your child may take longer to develop the skills of first identifying what her body is feeling, and then asking for help with an intervention.

One Saturday morning a few years back, Will skipped breakfast because he wasn't hungry, and since we were on the go, I forgot to feed him lunch. By mid-afternoon, he was a monster and had a full-tilt meltdown in the supermarket because I wouldn't buy him Lunchables for school the next week. Then it dawned on me. Duh, Mom! The kid is starving. When I asked him if he was hungry, he retorted, "Of course, I am! I'm starving." When I asked him why he hadn't told me, he said, "Well, you should have known!" And maybe I should have.

Kids with AS have other, more complex, types of tantrums. In second grade, Will participated in an after-school program called Science Adventures. He loved it; it was right up his alley, until one day I found him under a table in the multipurpose room at school screaming and in tears when I came in to pick him up. I asked the instructor what had happened, and she couldn't answer me: "He's been like that for 10 minutes, I have no idea what set him off!"

I got down on my hands and knees and dragged Will out from under the table. As he calmed down, he kept talking about "that picture" and asking if it was "real." I tried to get more information from him, and finally I figured out that he was talking about a picture on the table. I looked at it, and showed it to him. He started screaming again. "Is it real, Mommy?" he pleaded.

It was a picture of a dummied-up crime scene, with a "murder" victim on the ground and a weapon nearby. To the average kindergartner, the scene was obviously fake – the body was a mannequin, the gun was fake, and so on. To my AS child, it was a real dead body. As we talked about it, it became clear that to him the picture was the real thing; that is to say, that not only wasn't it fake, and not only was it a picture of the real thing, to him it was the thing itself. He reacted to the picture the same way he would have reacted to a real dead body in the class, much in the way very small children won't touch a picture of a snake for fear of being bitten. He could not discern between fakery, representation, and reality. All of the lines were blurred. He was scared to death. No wonder the kid had a tantrum!

Getting Help

If your child has issues with aggression, tantrums, or acting-out behaviors, you may want to read and use *Asperger Syndrome and Difficult Moments* by Brenda Smith Myles and Jack Southwick (2005). If the behaviors don't go away with at-home interventions, I strongly urge you to seek professional help. All kids, indeed all humans, can act out in response to very complicated psychological stresses, and it may well be beyond your ability as a parent to get to the bottom of his problem. And while you may be able to curb the behavior or symptom, if the underlying problem isn't dealt with directly, it may manifest in another type of destructive behavior.

Depressed Behavior

A common problem for children and adolescents with Asperger Syndrome is depression. Unable to cope with social rejection, under constant stress at school trying to figure out "the rules," it should come as no surprise that these children sometimes fall into a mild to severe depression. Depression may manifest in different ways and at different ages among boys and girls. Whereas boys tend to exhibit depression in equal numbers to girls prior to puberty, the onset of adolescence raises the incidence in girls dramatically. Further, the ways in which girls and boys demonstrate depression can be quite different. Often, boys manifest depression in an outward fashion, through aggressive acts, destructive behavior, and so forth. Girls, on the other hand, generally turn the depression inward, and may begin to disregard their personal safety or engage in self-destructive behaviors such as eating disorders.

Children with AS are often acutely aware that they are "different" from other children, that they have some sort of deficit (though they often cannot tell you what it is until well into intervention). Additionally, they crave social interaction, friendships, respect, and attention, and because of their social awkwardness, are often unable to attain the friends they so dearly desire. This can set them up to be prime candidates for depression, especially when an additional "stressor" such as changes in the family structure, change of school, or loss of a loved one is added to their lives.

Sadness and Listlessness

One of the primary symptoms of depression is a sad and blue mood lasting for more than a few days at a time or recurring frequently over time. Your child may be uninterested in doing the things she normally likes, she may be withdrawn and irritable. She may also say things like, "I don't know why I bother," "Nobody cares what I do anyway," or make other self-defeating statements.

While it is not unusual for all children to feel dejected and sad from time to time, the qualifier here is "over an extended period of time." If your child is just having a bad day, you can choose to try to buck her up a bit, or just ignore the behavior and have her work it out, as many children do. But if it continues for more than a few days, you need to start asking questions about what is happening in her world that is making her feel hopeless. You may get a direct and straightforward answer, like, "I'm doing badly in school" or "I can't make any friends," or you may get a litany of catastrophic "nevers," "always," "no ones," and "everyones": "No one likes me," "I never get invited anywhere," "I'm always the last one picked," and "Everyone has friends but me."

The first type of response is much easier to deal with – your child has told you directly what is wrong, and you can begin to start working on those issues with her. The second is harder, in that it points to a larger underlying problem of feelings of worthlessness and negativism.

You can try working on these issues yourself by validating her feelings ("I hear that you are really sad because you haven't been invited to a birthday party lately"), but at the same time offering evidence that her thinking is skewed ("But remember, two months ago you went to Jimmy's party and had a great time!"). If you can't pry her out of this "wrong" thinking, I highly recommend you read *The Optimistic Child* by Martin Seligman (1996), and *How to Talk So Kids Will Listen & How to Listen So Kids Will Talk* by Adele Faber and Elaine Mazlish (1999). Both are excellent books, and on my list of "Nine Books You Really Should Own" in the back of this book. And if the advice in those books does not help, or if your child is spiraling into a deeper depression, seek professional help. Clinical depression does not go away by itself. It must be treated.

Self-Destructive Behavior

Self-destructive behaviors, such as hitting oneself or destroying favorite toys (in younger children) and engaging in dangerous behaviors such as promiscuity, drug abuse, and lawlessness (in older children), are often symptoms of depression, and should be treated in much the same way as depressed behavior. The caution here is to ensure that your child does not pose a threat to himself or to others. If your child is talking about killing himself, or saying things like "No one wants me around anymore," have him seen immediately by a child psychologist or psychiatrist. While most talk of suicide is an attention-getting device, you cannot and should not take any chances.

When Will was in second grade, he began hitting himself on the forehead with a closed fist repeating, "I'm so stupid! I'm stupid! I'm stupid!" He would do this over the least little thing – forgetting to feed the cat, getting a "B-"on a spelling test, or forgetting to take a quarter to school for juice bar day. Clearly, these things were not the real issue – they merely provoked a response. Overall, he felt badly about himself, and was having a miserable time in school. It took a long time to work him out of this behavior, so he had more faith in himself and the world around him.

Certainly, if your child is expressing any self-mutilating behaviors such as cutting himself, biting himself, or burning himself, get immediate help. These are behaviors that point to a major internal breakdown, and your child needs professional help.

Low Self-Esteem

Along with, or part of, depression is often a feeling of low self-worth. This is an ongoing issue for many kids with AS, even if it does not evolve into clinical depression, so be vigilant in ensuring that your child feels as good about herself as possible. This may mean helping her cope with bullies at school, feel okay about any problems she has, selecting sports that she can feel confident in playing, and so forth. Your child needs to be successful at as many things as she reasonably can in order to build her self-esteem. Success breeds success: When she is masterful at one, two, or three things, other mastery comes more easily, and her deficits don't seem so huge any more in perspective. If she knows she can overcome one difficult problem, it will give her the confidence she needs to tackle another.

Getting Help

If your child is suffering from depression, seek professional help. A lot can and should be done in the home to scaffold your child, but it is sometimes hard to differentiate between a bad case of the blues and a full-blown case of depression. When in doubt, ask for help.

Cheap Tricks
for Unwanted Behaviors

While little short of professional intervention may help for depression and raging behaviors, milder behaviors can be temporarily thwarted in a pinch while working toward longer-term solutions. Just as with "regular" parenting (whatever that is), diversion tactics often do the trick.

✋ Don't Forget the Obvious

Kids get hungry at the most inopportune moments. Keep snacks and juice boxes in your car and purse. Also, plan your trips and your visits to friends and family at times when your child is not usually tired. Well-rested, well-fed children are always happier.

✋ Favorite Fidgets

If your child needs sensory stimulation to maintain composure, especially in new situations, keep a stash of Wikki Stiks (soft wax sticks that can be manipulated), Koosh balls, Silly Putty or other non-messy manipulatives in your purse or car. A child quietly playing with a Koosh ball in a corner of your Aunt Mabel's living room may seem a bit odd to your extended family, but it's a lot less disruptive than having him screaming at the top of his lungs that he wants to go home and watch Pokémon videos.

> ✋ **Stash of Treats**
>
> Call me materialistic, but when Will was young I kept a stash of small toys in the closet for emergencies when he melted down and nothing would console him and for whatever reason I couldn't cope with his behavior at that moment. Things like mini-Lego sets, small bags of plastic dinosaurs, coloring books, and the like – nothing expensive, just small treats that would divert him temporarily with their novelty. Yes, after a while he began asking for these treats, and you're right, it did nothing to help the root cause of his behaviors, but sometimes just getting through the moment was enough to complete a phone call or finish signing escrow papers to refinance the house.
>
> ✋ **Silly Songs and Games**
>
> Another wonderful diversion tactic is to sing songs or play a quick game. Anything from singing Old MacDonald using wilder and wilder farm animals (a platypus on a farm?) to playing "I Spy" on the road will work. As Will got older, one of our favorite road trips became making silly sentences out of the letters on license plates, such as XUP 123 – Xylophones Unzip Penguins!

References

Faber, A., & Mazlish, E. (1999). *How to talk so kids will listen & how to listen so kids will talk.* New York: Avon Books.

Gray, C. (1993). *The original Social Story™ book.* Arlington, TX: Future Horizons.

Gray, C. (1994). *The new Social Story™ book*. Arlington, TX: Future Horizons.

Gray, C. (2002). *My Social Stories™ book*. London: Jessica Kingsley Publishers.

Kazimi, M. (1996). *Gender and depression*. Retrieved October 16, 2006, from http://www.mit.edu/~womens-studies/writingPrize/mk96.html

Kranowitz, C. (2006). *The out-of-sync child*. New York: The Berkeley Publishing Group.

Lynn, G. (2007). *The Asperger plus child – How to identify and help children with Asperger Syndrome and seven common co-existing conditions*. Shawnee Mission, KS: Autism Asperger Publishing Company.

MedlinePlus, U.S. National Library of Medicine and National Institutes of Health. (n.d.). *Adolescent depression*. Retrieved October 16, 2006, from http://www.nlm.nih.gov/medlineplus/ency/article/001518.htm

Myles, B., Cook, K. T., Miller, N.E., Rinner, L., & Robbins, L. A. (2000). *Asperger Syndrome and sensory issues: Practical solutions for making sense of the world*. Shawnee Mission, KS: Autism Asperger Publishing Company.

Myles, B. S., & Southwick, J. (2005). *Asperger Syndrome and difficult moments: Practical solutions for tantrums, rage, and meltdowns*. Shawnee Mission: Autism Asperger Publishing Company.

Obeidallah, D., & Earls, F. (1999). *Adolescent girls: The role of depression in delinquency*. National Institute of Justice Research Preview. Retrieved October 16, 2006, from http://www.ncjrs.gov/pdffiles1/fs000244.pdf

Seligman, M. (1996). *The optimistic child*. New York: HarperCollins.

Chapter 11

Family Time

School may have a major impact on a child's life on a daily basis, but family is the nurturing nest that children return to each day to rejuvenate, relax, and refresh. And just as working parents thrill to walk through the door each evening to their safe retreat, so should your child.

But often, family time is hectic. We are stretched too thin, doing too much, just trying to keep up. If family time is supposed to be so wonderful, why does it seem we are we fighting a lot of the time?

Help! My Kid Is Driving Me Wild!

Being a parent is one of the most challenging jobs you will ever have, and raising a child with AS can be doubly, or triply, challenging. Not only are you a parent, a nurse, a coach, and a tutor, you may also be taking on the role of therapist, speech pathologist, IEP administrator, educational advocate, and AS specialist. It can be a tough job.

If you are struggling with your child, you may have turned to this chapter first. If that's the case, or if you've merely skimmed through the first part of this book, I encourage you to go back and read the rest of the book thoroughly. Then, once you've begun to understand what makes your child tick (or tock in this case), and have tried interventions for some of the low-hanging symptoms, keep reading.

Looking at Your Child Holistically

One of the things that I failed at early on was to look at my child holistically. Because his problems and presenting symptoms were so overwhelming, I spent most of my time interacting with him as a tutor or teacher, helping him learn social skills.

What I missed during that time was a fun, wonderful, and exceptional child who had many strengths beyond his deficits. If I had spent more time playing with him, reading books to him, and being silly with him, maybe his deficits wouldn't have seemed so overwhelming to me. It's something for you to consider. Our children are far more than their diagnosis, and we need to be mindful of that.

Your Unfulfilled Expectations

Along with looking at your child as a whole person, you need to examine your own unfulfilled expectations. This process doesn't get enough attention, in my opinion. Having a child with special needs means that something has been lost, no matter how minor, and as parents, we need to be respectful of our own need to grieve over the loss of "normalcy" (whatever that means).

If you were really good in sports as a child, it may be difficult for you to raise a child who is clumsy, awkward, and fears any type of sport. You may be grieving for a lost chance to interact with your child in something that is important to you, something you had as a child.

If you were very social and popular as a child, it may be difficult for you to have a shy and socially withdrawn child who has few friends. You may have fond memories of neighborhood kids running in and out of your house, sleepovers, birthday parties and the like – experience that your child doesn't have, at least not to the same extent.

This can be painful, and it will likely bring up feelings of loss and grief. It may also make you a "super parent," who will try anything to achieve for her child what she had as a child herself, because we tend to equate our happiness in childhood with our children's happiness. Whether we like it or not, we have a strong tendency to live through our children. This is partly because we are so psychically and emotionally linked to them that it is sometimes hard to recognize and respect boundaries between ourselves and our offspring.

What is important to remember here is that although we have the right to grieve over our loss, we must make sure that we are not trying to remake our children into ourselves or into some idealized, socially approved child, without regard for his or her individuality. Seeing your child holistically instead of as a set of symptoms goes a long way. Look at the strengths you can encourage her to develop. Look at what interests her; what she is passionate about. Look at what she is already masterful at. There is so much in any child, if we only try to find it.

If your child is truly driving you wild, you may need to examine your expectations. Is it possible that he's driving you crazy because he isn't the type of child you had dreamed you'd be raising one day? Is it possible that the problem lies more in what you want him to be rather than with who he is?

He's Just a Kid

One of the key issues that we tend to overlook as parents of children with AS is that they are just kids. I don't know how many times I thought I was meeting with yet another presentation of AS symptoms in Will, when after talking to parents of other kids I discovered that it was just a generalized developmental phase. The latest of these is the hand on the hip, the disgusted look, and the phrase, "Mom, really!" Take pleasure in these moments – he's right on track!

I encourage you to expand your child's social horizons (as well as your own) beyond children with special needs and their families. It can lend a lot of balance to the equation for all involved, and will give you feedback on what kids are doing at any given age. Such feedback will help you to set parameters and to see where your child is fitting in or not fitting in. Plus, there is great comfort in knowing that in many ways your child is just like everyone else.

Lightening the Load

One of the most common triggers I've seen for meltdowns at home, both with Asperger kids and non-Asperger kids, is having a schedule that is too demanding. We cram so much into our lives that it's amazing we are not all running around with panic attacks, obsessive-compulsive behaviors, and nervous breakdowns. Swimming, soccer, baseball, hockey, math tutoring, language tutoring, Scouts, playdates, camps, enrichment programs, after-school care – it's too much. Kids don't have much time to be kids any more, and after being dragged around to their own extracurricular stuff (as well as any sibling's), it's no wonder they have no energy to do much besides watching TV and playing Nintendo.

Not only are we living frenetic lives, we are imposing this lifestyle on our children, and often to their detriment. If you can, cut back on the activities your child and your family participate in. Select one or two for each child, no more. Don't feel you have to accept every invitation to do something. Sometimes just giving kids space to be kids is all that is needed to reduce tension in the home. Send them outside to play. Take them to the park – without the GameBoys.

If life at home is especially hectic because you're a single mom or a double-income family, find as many ways as you can to use your time efficiently (make all sandwiches on Sunday and freeze them; cut up all veggies and fruit in advance) so that you can also sit and play – with your kids, and by yourself! If you are always on the go, running from one place to another, doing 16 things at once until 10 p.m., then collapsing in bed only to start over again at 6 a.m., that's what your child will learn.

There are many things you can do to help keep family time less stressful by putting simple tools in place at home. One of the best books available for creating a peaceful, pleasant environment is *Finding Our Way: Practical Solutions for Creating a Supportive Home and Community for the Asperger Syndrome Family* by Kristi Sakai (2005). This book is filled with great ideas and tips about how to build a family system that works for everyone.

As important as it is for your children to be kids, it is equally important that you get some time to just goof off. Model a balanced life. Not only will you reap rewards, but your children will learn that life is not all about work and busy-ness.

Breakdown Ahead

If you've read this far and none of this seems to apply to you and your situation, maybe it's time to look elsewhere. If you are engaging in ongoing power struggles, if your child can't hold to a simple schedule no matter how much scaffolding you put in place, if she is having major tantrums and you cannot find any reason for them, then I recommend that you reach out for help. Some children are so affected, and some families are so ingrained in given patterns, that it may take a professional to help sort it all out.

Remember that your child, if she truly has AS, is very unlikely to be acting out of defiance or maliciousness. These kids simply are not wired this way. There is something wrong, and she needs help.

Mom and Dad – Divided or United?

Nearly every married couple has areas where they don't agree – whether it's over what to serve for dinner, where to go on the family vacation, whether to invest money or build an addition. There are constant adjustments, readjustments, and conciliation.

Add to that the difficulty of raising a child with special needs, and the effects on Mom and Dad's relationship can be devastating. While you don't have to agree on everything, you will need to agree to disagree in order to keep marital peace.

Co-Parenting Challenges

Figuring out how to co-parent can be challenging. Both you and your spouse have certain ideals about parenting, along with fond and negative memories about your own upbringing. Add to that the fact that most of us are woefully undereducated about how to parent – frankly, it's a wonder that any of our children make it to something that looks like sane, well-adjusted, adulthood.

I'm going to make a prediction here. Whoever in your family is reading this passage first is the person to whom the majority of the "work" in raising the children has fallen in the past. You are likely the one who sought out a diagnosis for your child, the one who has been going to the IEP meetings, and the one who works with your child's teachers, specialists, therapists, and so on. Research shows that you are likely the Mom, hence the title of this book (and my sincere apologies – and kudos – to all the Dads who bought this book and are reading it first).

My point in making this prediction is to simply tell you that, like the rest of the world, one of the two of you probably tends to be more involved and more proactive in this area of your child's life. Talk to your friends, and you will see similar patterns in other families. Blame it on societal roles, hardwiring, whatever, just know that it is typical – and okay.

Given this, you and your spouse may have very different ideas of what it means to parent a child, and having a child with AS may make these differences even more pronounced. This is not necessarily a bad thing, but you both need to come to respect each other's viewpoints on how to cope with raising an AS child. If you don't talk about it together, if you ignore these differences, you may unconsciously undermine the parenting goals the other is trying to accomplish.

A Note About Denial

I've seen a couple of families where one parent seems to disbelieve that there is anything different about their child and works to undermine any interventions that the other parent puts in place. This is harmful for everyone involved. If you truly feel that your spouse is denying the existence of a problem or is minimizing it to a large degree, I suggest you consider getting into couple's counseling. This type of disagreement can undermine your marriage. It will also undermine any help that you can secure for your child.

Allowing for Differences

In any co-parenting situation, both parents must be cognizant and respectful of difference in style. Being a laid-back parent doesn't make you uninvolved, nor does being a very involved parent make you overinvolved. If the two of you are very different, this will likely play out in your parenting, including your parenting of your AS child.

One of the best pieces of advice I can give is to learn from your partner's way of doing things. If you are really laid back, have never read a book on Asperger Syndrome or parenting, sit back and watch the kids rather than play with them, maybe it's a good idea to get up and take a more pro-active role. If, on the other hand, you are constantly on the go, involved with every aspect of your child's life, reading every book and taking every seminar related to her challenges, maybe you should take a page from your spouse's book and take a breather.

Not only should we allow for differences, we should take the opportunity to learn from them. This process can have a curative effect on any family or couple in stress.

Your Spouse's Unfulfilled Expectations

Like you, your spouse has unfulfilled expectations regarding raising a child with special needs. And like you, he or she needs to be given the space to experience this grief. If my prediction above was true and you are the Mom reading this, I'll make another prediction: Your husband may be unaware that he is saddened and grieving for the child he didn't have.

Talk to your spouse about it. If he or she is unwilling to talk at first, talk about your own feelings of loss. This type of disclosure often helps open up people to look inside and share what they feel.

While not the most admirable of human reactions, a child with AS can cause us embarrassment, especially when we are out in a world that doesn't understand her. We can be embarrassed because she talks too loudly or too long, she lies on the floor of a restaurant tantruming, she picks at her food and complains that it tastes bad. We can be embarrassed when our child misses an "easy" catch in softball and then bursts into tears. We can be embarrassed when all the other children play tag at school Open House night and our child hangs on the periphery, talking to herself.

All of this can take a huge psychic toll if not addressed. Both parents need to accept it, grieve, and learn new ways to be proud of their exceptional child.

The Untold Stress

Having a child can be stressful under the best of circumstances. Having a child with special needs usually adds further stress. Time may be short due to special classes and interventions that your child needs and the extra work it takes just to get through the day-to-day activities of life.

Money may be short because of the cost of special camps, therapies not covered by insurance, and special education extras that your child needs. Patience may be short as you try to juggle a million balls, put out the proverbial fires, and just get through.

If you add the stress of very different parenting styles or very different modes of operation, you may be setting yourself up for fights, adult temper tantrums, alcohol and drug abuse, depression, anxiety attacks, or divorce.

Note:

The kind of chronic stress that raising a child with special needs entails can affect relationships at their weakest points. According to the U.S. Census Bureau (2000), 47% of first marriages fail and 57% of all marriages end in divorce. Although the findings are inconsistent, there is general consensus among experts that while the divorce rates are comparable, there appears to be more reported marital distress among families of children with special needs. (Seligman, M., & Darling, R. [1999]. *Ordinary families, special children*. New York: Guilford Press.)

Without a good foundation, respect, and established ways to work through conflict together, marriages can easily fail with the addition of a special needs kid. Whenever possible, your child needs an intact family unit. He needs both of you, and you need your spouse to get through this. Work on yourself, work on your marriage. It will benefit you all.

Be a Couple – At Least Some of the Time

As with any busy family, it is not possible to always put family first. While this makes sense most of the time, if you don't make time for yourself and for each other, there may be little family left in a few years.

Get away with your spouse. Get good babysitters, and go out to dinner – once a week, once every other week – even if it's to your favorite burger joint. If you can afford it, take a vacation alone together, maybe just a weekend to your favorite getaway. Having trouble finding good babysitters? Go back to your network of other AS families and ask to swap babysitting services. Ask for referrals for mature undergraduate or graduate students at the local college or university. Sure, the kids may miss you while you're gone, maybe the school projects won't get done, and maybe the cat doesn't get fed one day. Big deal.

Be good to your marriage or partnership. Remember why you fell in love. Learn to respect all over again if need be. Be forgiving and kind and loving. Laugh. Everyone needs a best friend when times are tough.

Therapy for Mom and Dad

Therapy can be a very useful tool for parents who are stressed, tired, and grouchy. While most couples will probably never need therapy to survive, I think that a lot of couples could benefit from therapy to live well.

If your marriage is showing signs of strain that plain old rekindling isn't addressing, hie thee to a good couple's counselor and work on the marriage. I'm big on whole families wherever possible, especially with kids with special needs in the picture. And I believe it to be a worthwhile expedition to work on the marriage rather than throw it away.

Sibling Warfare

If you have more than one child, you know that having an AS child can put the rest of the family at odds. The family balance may inadvertently be shifted toward the child with AS, or it may inadvertently be shifted to another child in the family. Or, if the family is really suffering, Mom and Dad may be under such stress that all of the children are more or less on their own.

Too Much Attention or Not Enough?

It is difficult for the entire family not to center around the child with special needs. Her needs may be greater and more apparent, her behavior may take more work, her schoolwork might take more effort, and so forth. This is especially true in a family where the other children are very high functioning, and can get by with very little intervention from the parents.

If this describes your family, be cautioned that there may be underlying issues that may not have surfaced. And, if you've already seen some "inexplicable" blow-ups from your child's siblings, you may already have gotten a taste of the hurt and anger that the typical kids feel because their brother or sister with AS has taken up so much emotional and psychic energy.

I've even heard stories where younger children develop "symptoms" of AS or behavioral issues in direct response to their older sibling's difficult passage through life. We as parents can become so attuned to the needs of our special kid that we jump every time he starts to teeter – and sometimes to the detriment of the other children in our care.

Siblings can get jealous of the attention their brother or sister with AS gets, and often find ways (unconsciously or consciously) to demand more attention from Mom and Dad. For this reason, make sure that all of your children get as equal a share of your time and resources as humanly possible. And don't think that by telling his older sister, "Gee Sue, you're so talented and gifted in everything you do, I know I can trust you to do this whole science project without my help," you are bolstering her self-esteem, especially if you spent hours helping her brother on a similar project the month before.

Kids keep track. And while Sue might well be able to do the entire project herself, what she may hear is "You don't need me as much as your brother does." Of course, she does! Develop time in your schedule so that each child, if at all possible, gets some alone time with Mom and Dad. Focus on your other children's "deficits," don't let them slide because they don't seem as important as your AS child's issues. If Sue really wants to try out for softball and needs help with batting, it makes sense to skip a speech therapist appointment to take her to a batting cage.

If you become slavish to the needs of your AS child, all of your other children will suffer and become jealous and angry at both you and your AS kid.

A Final Word About Praise

Try not to use empty praise for any of your children's efforts, and try to never hold up one child's work to another child as an example of how it should be done. Empty praise rings false on everyone's ears, and no one likes to be reminded that so-and-so did a better job than she did. Instead, use concrete feedback ("You really followed the instructions well!") and encouragement ("Studying for your test really paid off – you got a great grade!). This is far more meaningful feedback to a child than "You are so smart, you can do anything without my help!"

Teaching Differences

When your children are old enough to realize that their brother or sister with AS is different (maybe as early as 6 or 7 or as late as 10 or 12), begin to introduce the concept of differing abilities to his siblings. Depending on the birth order, this may happen as soon as you get a diagnosis, or much later.

It's important to use age-appropriate language when talking to young children, and even with older children it's a good idea to introduce the concepts slowly, lest they think that there is something terribly wrong with their brother, and begin to worry unnecessarily. You can modify the scripts in the section Age-Appropriate Information and use them with your child's siblings.

Telling all of your children about your child with AS is an invaluable lesson in tolerance and accepting differences in others. Don't let this lesson go unused, thinking that your other children won't ever need to know. By the same token, it's a good idea to inform your children that this type of information is best kept inside the family, and then list specifically who they might talk to about their sibling's issues.

Don't be surprised (or upset) if your younger children "blab" about this to other kids or adults. They may need to test the information out with others to see how it is received. That's okay. Remember that you are most concerned with how your family deals with the issue, not with how others deal with it.

Setting Boundaries for All Children

That all children need boundaries is conventional wisdom, and yet it is wisdom that often gets lost in the fray when a child with special needs enters the picture. Whether your

AS child is constantly picking on his older sister, or whether your daughter is calling him an idiot at every opportunity, you need to step in.

Having AS is not an excuse for bad behavior. It is a set of presenting symptoms that makes certain social interactions, cognitive processes, and physical control more difficult, but that's it. Even though it is harder to teach children with AS "manners" and The Golden Rule, that doesn't mean that they should be exempt from general social graces. On the contrary: It means that they need such instruction more than most kids.

Do not make excuses for your AS child to his siblings. Don't be tempted to say to his older sister, for example, "Well, that's just how Joe is. We have to accept it," because guess what? She will not accept it, and neither should you, and what she will see is that there are different sets of boundaries for the children in your family. This alone will create a sense of unfairness in your home, and create resentment in your other children.

It is fine to tell your AS child's siblings that "Joe has a harder time remembering the rules of the house" or that "Sometimes Joe acts before he thinks. We need to work harder to help him remember what he is supposed to do." There should be an equal and level set of expectations in your home for all children (depending on their ages, of course), and all children should be expected to toe the line. Remember that the world can be a cold place, and a future college teacher, employer, spouse, or friend may not cut your child slack because he has Asperger Syndrome.

If the sibling fracas is coming from the "typical" children in your family, use the teaching moment to work on tolerance. Kids with AS may take longer to learn social graces, and this may be a source of frustration, especially to older siblings. Set firm boundaries in your family on name-calling (not allowed!) and how to deal with frustration and anger (with words, not with fists!). No matter how frustrated your other children are, work with them to ensure that they don't belittle or demean their sibling with AS. The last thing the child needs is more social ostracizing, especially in the one place where he should be emotionally safe to be who he is – in his home.

In many ways, his siblings are the best allies your AS child has. In most families, there is a built-in tolerance factor, where kids are aware that they can't walk away from troubling situations (as much as they may want to). In the best of circumstances, your AS child's siblings are the primary grit that smoothes off his rough edges – he may learn more about social interaction from them than from anyone else.

Remember – They're Kids

Do remember that all of your children are just kids, and that bickering, occasional name-calling, and major blowups will occur. That's how real life is, and every scramble your children get into will teach them how to interact better with each other – what works and what doesn't. Whenever possible, let them try to work things out on their own, and to be the best kids that they can be in every way.

The Extended Family and Close Friends

If you're lucky, your children don't live in a world unto themselves, but have extended family and friends in the vicinity. Raising a child with special needs can be an isolating experience, in that it is difficult to bring a child to a family function who doesn't behave like his cousins and friends.

Parents can become isolated just from the sheer magnitude of the effort it takes to keep a family with a special needs kid on track. It can often be hard to find time to be with our extended family and close friends, unless we make a conscious effort to do so.

What the Grandparents (and Aunts, Uncles, and Close Friends) Need to Know

If your children have grandparents alive, or better yet, extended family living close enough so that you can visit them frequently, count yourself blessed. But whether your children's extended family lives next door or 5,000 miles a way, they can be great mentors to your children, and help to you and your partner.

However, you may find that the relationship is a bit strained from time to time if your child consistently acts differently or inappropriately when around family or friends. It is wise, therefore, to share enough information with your family and close friends so that they know that you are aware that there are issues. Sadly, extended family can be a bit catty and assume that your child's inability to handle social functions seamlessly is due to poor parenting. Additionally, if you take an instructive approach to shaping your child's behavior rather than a more traditional, punitive one, you may be seen as spoiling your child.

The best way to combat this type of thinking in your family is to explain that your child has Asperger Syndrome, and tell them what that means: He has certain social deficits and cognitive processing challenges that make traditional family gatherings more stressful for him than for other children. Lend them this book, if it makes sense. I would take aside close family friends and tell them the same thing. Everyone will have figured out that there is something different about your child anyway. What you are doing is giving that "something" a name, and explaining what it means.

I also encourage you to talk to the parents of close friends or relatives who have children who interact with yours on a regular basis, and ask them to speak to their children about your child's issues. While this is a very sensitive area, you might frame it as giving these parents the opportunity to work with their own children to build tolerance in them. This is a vital life lesson that we all need to learn. If these are truly close and trusted friends, you are not burdening them. Instead, look at it as giving these friends the gift of a useful and important teaching moment for their children.

Everyone Knows Better Than You

One of the common pitfalls of having close friends and family is that you may be the target of well-meaning, but sometimes unwelcome, advice. I've heard of grandparents who refuse to admit that there is anything amiss in their grandchild with AS that a little firm discipline wouldn't cure, or who insist that the child be removed from public school altogether and sent to a special school where things will be easier for the child.

Take this advice with a grain of salt – and maybe even consider the validity of it before throwing it away completely (maybe a special school would be the best thing for your child). But do remain confident that you see your child as no one else does – holistically – and that you and your partner are in a much better position to ensure that his needs are met. If family members continue to pester you about how you are raising your child, consider taking them to talk to a specialist in AS. It might cost you the price of a session, but it may earn you a great deal of peace in the family. Often, we listen to experts when we refuse to listen to each other.

Finally, if these family members or friends refuse to "get it" and continue to make trouble, you may simply need to limit contact with them.

Building Special Time

All families need special gathering times, whether it's the nuclear family getting together for a Seder, or it's 24 extended-family members coming over for Thanksgiving. These times are precious for all children, and even though your child with AS may have a difficult time staying in his seat at the dinner table, don't forego these activities.

Set expectations with the rest of the attendees in advance, if possible. For example, if your wiggle worm can't sit still and you're going to your mother-in-law's house for Grampa's birthday party, tell her that you are allowing your child to get up and run around outside between each course, and then after dinner and before birthday cake. Suggest that since your young AS child cannot resist "helping" to open someone's birthday present, maybe Grampa can let each child help with one present.

Thinking through the potential challenges in advance, and having a plan (or two or three) at the ready to avert disaster, is well worth the time. If everyone's on the same page, you have the added benefit of support for the rules you set forth with your child.

Making Peace

As expectant parents, most of us dreamed of wonderful, happy moments that we would spend with our partners and children. Even in the best of circumstances, these fantasies rarely play out, due to constraints of time, money, patience, and the like. But that doesn't mean that your life at home has to be chaotic or unfulfilling. Everyone deserves to have a safe and nurturing sanctuary, especially you and your children.

Every Family Is Special

There is no recipe for what makes a family a family. Families come in all shapes and sizes, all colors, creeds, and ethnicities. Books and seminars abound on how to make family time special. Just remember that no matter how your family is constituted, it's a very special place to come into each day. Honor it as you would a cherished friend.

Every Family Member Is Special

As mentioned earlier, it's important that every person in the family has nearly equal access to Mom and Dad. Whether this means having a boys' night out or having the girls watch a chick-flick and do their nails is up to you, but remember that each child needs lots of attention, not just your child with AS.

This also means that Mom and Dad need time to be together and to be alone. If you have a hobby that has languished, or have always wanted to take an art class or get a degree, see if there is any way you can work in something just for you. Not only does it recharge your batteries, it also teaches all of your children that their happiness is in their own hands.

My own experience is that it's very difficult, but not impossible, to balance all of the individual and group aspects of family life. Although I enjoy giving to others and keeping my family moving on track, if I don't spend time doing the things I want to pursue (like writing a book), I feel like I'm being cheated out of something. As the saying goes, "If Mamma ain't happy, ain't nobody happy!"

Making Room for Family Fun, Routines, and Traditions

I'm big on traditions. I love looking forward to fall so we can buy pumpkins at the local farm where we have been going for years. I enjoy turning out a huge feast for my family on Thanksgiving. At Christmas, we make "necessity bags" and deliver them to the local homeless shelter. I love going out in early spring, turning the soil, and planting my first tomatoes.

Children with AS, especially with their love of schedules, tend to be big on traditions, too. So I encourage you to either maintain the traditions you have in your family, or create some new ones. Not only are they comforting to your child with special needs, they are enormously regenerative to the entire family. They don't have to be stodgy or "traditional" traditions – they can be as loony as you like. Maybe Wacky Hair Day on April Fools? Playing miniature golf on Mom's birthday? Whatever it is, getting together as a family to do things together helps build a bond between your AS child and his siblings that will last long after your life.

Traditions can be very simple. Pancakes after church on Sunday, going to Story Hour at the library on Friday nights, walking the dog after dinner together. Though your children may not view these events as "special" now, they will remember them in this way when they are older. Think of it as investing in their memory banks, making warm deposits every day.

Cheap Tricks for Family Time

This chapter is filled with all sorts of tricks you can use to keep your family close and loving, but here's a quick cheat sheet of ideas.

✋ Ask for Help

Don't think you have to do it all alone. If you have family nearby, ask them for help. If you have sympathetic neighbors, ask if your child can come over and play for 30 minutes once a week. Make friends with other families with special needs kids and swap time. If you can afford it, find babysitters and household help to lighten the load.

✋ Mom and Dad Time

If you're lucky enough to be part of an intact family, do your best to stay that way! Make time for your partner. Go out to dinner, take short vacations together. Although your family may be the pivotal focus most of the time, it shouldn't be the focus all of the time. Be grownups together and do grownup things.

✋ Time for Each Child

In any family with a child with special needs, the natural inclination is to focus the majority of its energy on that child. Needless to say, this is detrimental for all other children in the family if it goes on for a long period of time. Make sure that you as parents spend as much time with your other children as you do with your Asperger kid – over time. I've seen more than one family where, after focusing on a child with special needs, a "normal" sibling completely blows apart emotionally or psychologically. Remember that this isn't consciously manipulative behavior on the child's part – it's a basic survival skill all humans possess to get adults to parent all of their children equally.

✋ Don't Let Any ONE Person Control the Family

Related to the above, remember that a family unit needs to pool all resources and, as far as possible, dole them out evenly across the entire family. This means that whenever possible one child should not monopolize all of the family's time and money. Do what you can, when you can, to be fair to all of your children.

✋ Establish Traditions, Have Fun

Kids with Asperger Syndrome love routine and tradition anyway, so establishing set routines for birthdays, Hanukkah, trips to Uncle Bob's will comfort him. The side benefit is that it will also build loving memories in all of your children. I shouldn't have to say too much about having fun, but … so many of us (myself included) forget how trivial much of life is – to the extent of excluding fun. Being a kid – any kid – should be fun much of the time. It's not a bad way to go for us parents, either!

References

Ariel, C., & Naseef, R. (2006). *The relationship factor: When special needs challenges a household.* Retrieved October 16, 2006, from www.specialfamilies.com/special_couples.htm

Sakai, K. (2005). *Finding our way: Practical solutions for creating a supportive home and community for the Asperger Syndrome family.* Shawnee Mission: Autism Asperger Publishing Company.

Seligman, M., & Darling, R. (1997). *Ordinary families, special children.* New York: Guilford Press.

Afterword

The Bigger Picture

Now that we've gone through some of the minutiae of helping a child with AS, it's time to stand back a bit and remember why we are here.

As a parent, your job is to guide your child through the stages of her life, providing support, love, correction, respect, and modeling of the values and beliefs that are important to you and your family. With a child with AS, your role is no different – the way you carry it out is slightly modified.

The end goal is the same: We all want our children to be healthy, happy adults, who can function in society to the highest level they can attain. We want our children to be productive members of society, holding down jobs, and obeying the law. We want our children to be good friends, good parents, and contributors to their communities. We want them to be responsible, forgiving, and loving. All of this means that our job is to do our best to ensure that our children go out into the world as self-actualized and self-supporting adults.

Afterword

So even when you're fighting over how long your child has played Nintendo today, or trying to figure out what type of intervention might help him finish a theme paper on time, try to remember the big picture. If the goal is to become a kind, useful adult, how important is each battle? Keeping an eye on the big picture will help you focus on what your child really needs from you.

In the end, children brought up in tolerant, respectful, and loving families will be great adults. Far more important than any intervention, any IEP, any activity you do with your child is the love you show for him each and every day.

With constant love, any child can flourish.

Resources & References

This section contains the following:

- ❏ The Nine Books You Should Own

- ❏ Useful Addresses and Websites

- ❏ Sample IEP Letters

- ❏ Complete Bibliography

The Nine Books You Should Own

This list comprises nine books that I think all parents of a child with AS should buy and have at their disposal. I have relied heavily on all of them for the material for this book, and continue to refer to them time and again while parenting my own child.

1) ***The Out-of-Sync Child***, Carol Stock Kranowitz, Perigee Books, 2006.
   This is an excellent book that fully describes sensory integration deficit, which commonly affects children with AS, NLD, and autism. A great resource.

2) ***Asperger Syndrome and Sensory Issues – Practical Solutions for Making Sense of the World***, Brenda Smith Myles, Katherine Tapscott Cook, Nancy E. Miller, Louann Rinner, and Lisa A. Robbins, AAPC, 2000.
   This book has wonderful interventions for children who have sensory issues, and is written in a fun and engaging way. It includes sensory screening checklists, which can help you identify what areas your child may need help in.

3) *The Complete IEP Guide*, Lawrence Siegel, Nolo Press, 1999.
   This book covers all aspects of an IEP from start to finish. It takes a fairly dim view of school districts and is somewhat adversarial, but it is an incredibly useful book to read thoroughly and then have on hand for questions about your child's IEP.

4) *Good Friends Are Hard to Find*, Fred Frankel and Barry Wetmore, Perspective Publishing, 1996.
   This is an exceptional book, useful for all parents who have children who don't quite fit in. The authors describe developmentally appropriate social interactions in boys and girls (who behave quite differently), discuss where issues are likely to occur in friendship making, and offer step-by-step interventions for teaching your child to be a good friend.

5) *How to Talk So Kids Will Listen & Listen So Kids Will Talk*, Adele Faber and Elaine Mazlish, Collins, 1999.
   Every parent should own this book. It gives practical, easy-to-read advice on how to have meaningful exchanges with your children.

6) *The Optimistic Child*, Martin Seligman, Harper Perennial Books, 1996.
   A great resource for parents of any child, this book includes exercises to determine how resilient your child is as well as exercises and advice on how to build resiliency in your child.

7) *Better IEPs: How to Develop Legally Correct and Educationally Useful Programs*, Barbara Bateman and Mary Anne Linden, Sopris West, 1998.
   This is an excellent resource to have on hand if you run into trouble getting a good, measurable IEP out of your school district.

8) *Asperger Syndrome and Difficult Moments – Practical Solutions for Tantrums, Rage and Meltdowns*, Brenda Smith Myles and Jack Southwick, AAPC, 2005.
   This book helps parents of AS children work through the "rage cycles" that so frequently plague these kids in constructive, workable ways.

9) *Finding Our Way: Practical Solutions for Creating a Supportive Home and Community for the Asperger Syndrome Family*, Kristi Sakai, AAPC, 2005.
   This heart-warming and positive resource offers excellent and easy-to-do strategies to help your child and your family fit into the outside world.

Useful Websites and Addresses

The following are websites and addresses that you might find useful over time. The Internet is notoriously volatile, so any of these sites may become defunct or move to another location without notice. Additionally, new websites on Asperger Syndrome and autism appear literally every day. Keep searching, and keep updating your browser's bookmarks.

http://www.asperger.org/
   This link will take you to a relatively new online resource, presented by MAAP. This site includes a phenomenal number of resources across the entire U.S., as well as articles, research reports, legal rights information, and more. Highly recommended.

www.udel.edu/bkirby/asperger/
   This link will take you to the OASIS (Online Asperger Syndrome Information and Support) site, which is

filled with up-to-date, useful resources, articles, links, and general information about the disorder.

http://www.tonyattwood.com.au/

If you have not heard of Tony Attwood, or read anything by him, plan on spending a few hours reviewing his site. It changes frequently, and there are always great articles and resources on this site.

www.autism-society.org

This is the Autism of America's Society site. It contains a great deal of information regarding social and educational policy around autism, and has a lot of useful references.

www.specialfamilies.com

This is an adjunct site to the Alternative Choices therapeutic clinic, and contains many good articles on what it means to be AS or autistic, as well as a good support network for parents who wish to pursue alternative interventions.

http://www.comeunity.com/disability/sensory_integration/

Part of the Come Unity website, this subsite has excellent resources on sensory integration, including an interview with Carol Kranowitz, author of the Out-of-Sync Child.

Professional Organizations

Use these organizations to locate a professional in your area who specializes in autism spectrum disorders.

American Psychological Association, Research Office and Education in Psychology and Accreditation Offices, 750 1st St. NE., Washington, DC 20002. http://www.apa.org

American Speech-Language-Hearing Association, 10801 Rockville Pike, Rockville, MD 20852. http://professional.asha.org

The American Occupational Therapy Association, 4720 Montgomery Ln., P.O. Box 31220, Bethesda, MD 20824-1220. http://www.aota.org

American Physical Therapy Association, 1111 North Fairfax St., Alexandria, VA 22314-1488. http://www.apta.org

American Bar Association, 750 North Lake Shore Dr., Chicago, IL 60611. http://www.abanet.org

Educational Advocates

You can locate an educational advocate by using one or more of these links.

http://www.a2zeducationaladvocates.com/

http://www.education-a-must.com/

http://www.successadvantage.com/Educational.htm

http://www.advocatesforchildren.org/links.php3

Sample Letters

The following section contains these sample letters for IEP correspondence:

- ❏ Letter requesting an initial IEP assessment
- ❏ Letter requesting an interim IEP meeting
- ❏ Letter requesting Due Process
- ❏ Letter filing a complaint

Letter Requesting an Initial IEP Assessment

August 4, 2007

Ms. Felicity Ranger, Special Education Director
Oakville School District
1000 Maple Street
Anytown, CA 95001

Dear Ms. Ranger:

I am writing you today to request that the Oakville School District provide my son Jonathan with an IEP assessment. Jonathan is entering third grade at Riverside Elementary School this year.

Jonathan was recently diagnosed as having Asperger Syndrome by Dr. Grande at Children's Hospital. The doctor has recommended that Jonathan receive in-school treatment and assistance. A copy of Dr. Grande's report is attached. I will make a second copy and request that it be included in Jonathan's school file at Riverside.

Please let me know the date of the initial IEP assessment as soon as you can. Thank you very much for your time.

Sincerely,

Jane Doe
1166 Oak Lane
Anytown, CA 95002

Letter Requesting an Interim IEP Meeting

October 21, 2007

Mr. Paul Stand, Resource Specialist
Oakville School District
1000 Maple Street
Anytown, CA 95001

Dear Mr. Stand:

I am writing you today as the administrator of Jonathan Doe's IEP
to request that you arrange an interim IEP meeting with me (his
mother), yourself, and Jonathan's classroom and speech teachers.

Jonathan has been having a very difficult time in class this last
month, and it has become clear to his teachers and me that we
need to arrange for different or additional interventions on his
behalf. He is unable to sit for any length of time, he cannot finish
his schoolwork, and he sits on the picnic table and cries throughout each lunch period. Additionally, his teacher reports that he is
unable to answer questions in a thoughtful manner, and constantly
interrupts her with "off-topic" questions when she is trying to
give a lesson.

Please let me know the date of the interim IEP meeting as soon as
you can so that we can work toward a more meaningful intervention
for Jonathan. Thank you very much for your time.

Sincerely,

Jane Doe
1166 Oak Lane
Anytown, CA 95002

Letter Requesting Due Process

March 30, 2007

Mr. Steven Sandleberg
Oakville County Education Office
2001 Big Street
Big City, CA 95012

Dear Mr. Sandleberg:

I am writing to request mediation with the Oakville School District with regard to my son Jonathan Doe. Jonathan is in third grade, and received a diagnosis of Asperger Syndrome last summer. While the district has placed Jonathan on an IEP, the interventions and services he is receiving are inadequate for his needs, and his teacher is at her wit's end.

Although I have repeatedly spoken to Mr. Stand (Jonathan's resource teacher) about the inadequacy of Jonathan's current interventions, specifically with regard to Jonathan's need of a full-time aide to help him through his day, Mr. Strand has not been forthcoming with appropriate help. Further attempts to work with Ms. Ranger, the special education director, have also been fruitless.

I have several emails from Jonathan's teacher (Mrs. White) indicating that she is unable to provide adequately for him during class. When Jonathan comes home each day from school, he throws one tantrum after another and cannot function enough to do his homework. Because this situation is getting worse and the district is not willing to help us, I find myself in need of exercising our rights to due process.

Sincerely,

Jane Doe
1166 Oak Lane
Anytown, CA 95002

Letter Filing a Complaint

April 13, 2007

Mr. Steven Sandleberg
Oakville County Education Office
2001 Big Street
Big City, CA 95012

Dear Mr. Sandleberg:

I am writing to file a formal complaint against the Oakville School District. My son Jonathan attends Riverside Elementary School, where he is in the third grade. Jonathan is on an IEP for difficulties he has in the school setting due to his Asperger Syndrome.

On March 24, I requested that the district administer the BRIEF behavioral assessment instrument, along with the NEPSY suite of tests. My letter to Ms. Ranger is attached. I have since heard from the district that they feel that Jonathan does not need these tests and that, therefore, the district will not administer them. I have contacted the district and informed them that this is not legal, but they have not answered my letters or phone calls.

Please let me know how I should properly file a complaint against Oakville in this matter.

Sincerely,

Jane Doe
1166 Oak Lane
Anytown, CA 95002

Complete Bibliography

American Psychiatric Association. (2000). *Diagnostic and statistical manual of mental disorders IV-TR* (4th ed.). Washington, DC: Author.

Ariel, C., & Naseef, R. (2006). *The relationship factor: When special needs challenges a household.* Retrieved October 16, 2006, from www.special-families.com/special_couples.htm

Arkwright, N. (1998). *An introduction to sensory integration.* Oxford, UK: The Psychological Corporation.

Asperger, H. (1944). Die "Autistischen Psychopathen" im Kindesalter. *Archiv fur Psychiatrie und Nervenkrankheiten, 117,* 76-136.

Asperger, H. *Hans Asperger.* Retrieved on December 30, 2006, from http://en.wikipedia.org/wiki/Hans_Asperger

Attwood, T. *Asperger's diagnostic assessment.* Retrieved on December 30, 2006, from http://www.tonyattwood.com.au/

Boon, R. *Asperger's Syndrome: Causes.* Retrieved October 16, 2006, from http://home.iprimus.com.au/rboon/Aspergers.htm

Cohen, D., & Volkmar, F. (2005). *Handbook of autism and pervasive developmental disorders.* New York: John Wiley & Sons.

Cohen, S. (1998). *Targeting autism.* Berkeley: University of California Press.

Cumine, V., Leach, J., & Stevenson, G. (1998). *Asperger Syndrome: A practical guide for teachers.* London: David Fulton Publishers.

Ehlers, S., & Gillberg, C. (1993, Nov). The epidemiology of Asperger Syndrome – A total population study. *Journal of Child Psychology and Psychiatry and Allied Disciplines, 34*(8), 1327-1350.

Faber, A., & Mazlish, E. (1999). *How to talk so kids will listen & how to listen so kids will talk.* New York: Avon Books.

Fling, E. (2000). *Eating an artichoke: A mother's perspective on Asperger Syndrome.* London: Jessica Kingsley Publishers.

Frankel, F., & Wetmore, B. (1996). *Good friends are hard to find.* Los Angeles: Perspective Publishing.

Free and appropriate public education. (n.d.). Retrieved December 30, 2006, from http://www.fapeonline.org/.

Frith, U. (2001, Dec.). *Mind blindness in the brain in autism. neuron, 32*(6), 969-979.

Frith, U. (Ed.). (1991). *Autism and Asperger syndrome.* Cambridge, UK: Cambridge University Press.

Gillberg, I. C., & Gillberg, C. (1989). Asperger syndrome- some epidemiological considerations: A research note. *Journal of Child Psychology and Psychiatry, 30,* 631-8.

Gray, C. (1993). *The original Social Story™ book*. Arlington, TX: Future Horizons.

Gray, C. (1994). *The new Social Story™ book*. Arlington, TX: Future Horizons.

Gray, C. (2002). *The sixth sense II*. New York: Free Spirit Publishing.

Gray, C. (2002). *My Social Stories™ book*. London: Jessica Kingsley Publishers.

Happé, F. (1994). *Autism: An introduction to psychological theory*. London: UCL Press.

Heinrichs, R. (2002). *Perfect targets: Asperger Syndrome and bullying: Practical Solution for surviving the social world*. Shawnee Mission, KS: Autism Asperger Publishing Company.

Jackson, P. (1968). *Life in classrooms*. New York: Teachers College Press.

Kanner, L., & Eisenberg, L. (1956). Early infantile autism 1943-1955. *American Journal of Orthopsychiatry, 26*, 55-65.

Kanner, L. *Leo Kanner*. Retrieved December 30, 2006, from. http://en.wikipedia.org/wiki/Leo_Kanner

Kazimi, M. (1996). *Gender and depression*. Massachusetts Institute of Technology. Retrieved October 16, 2006, from http://www.mit.edu/~womens-studies/writingPrize/mk96.html

Kennedy, R., Jr. (2005). *Deadly immunity*. Retrieved October 16, 2006, from http://dir.salon.com/story/news/feature/2005/06/16/thimerosal/print.html

Klin, A., & Volkmar, F. (1997). *Handbook of autism and pervasive developmental disorders* (2nd ed.). New York: John Wiley & Sons, Inc.

Kranowitz, C. (2006). *The out-of-sync child*. New York: The Berkeley Publishing Group.

LaSalle, B. (2004). *Finding Ben: A mother's journey through the maze of Asperger's*. New York: MacGraw Hill.

Learning Disabilities OnLine. *IDEA 2004*. Retrieved October 13, 2006, from www.ldonline.org

Lentz, K. (2004). *Hopes and dreams: An IEP guide for parents of children with autism spectrum disorders*. Shawnee Mission, KS: Autism Asperger Publishing Company.

Lynn, G. (2007). *The Asperger plus child – How to identify and help children with Asperger Syndrome and seven common co-existing conditions*. Shawnee Mission, KS: Autism Asperger Publishing Company.

MedlinePlus, U.S. National Library of Medicine and National Institutes of Health. *Adolescent depression*. Retrieved October 16, 2006, from http://www.nlm.nih.gov/medlineplus/ency/article/001518.htm

MRC Review of Autism Research: Epidemiology and Causes. (2001). *What are the causes of autism spectrum disorders?* (pp. 21-47). London: Medical Research Council.

Resources & References

Myles, B., Cook, K. T., Miller, N. E., Rinner, L., & Robbins, L. A. (2000). *Asperger Syndrome and sensory issues: Practical solutions for making sense of the world*. Shawnee Mission, KS: Autism Asperger Publishing Company.

Myles, B. S., & Southwick, J. (2005). *Asperger Syndrome and difficult moments: Practical solutions for tantrums, rage, and meltdowns* (rev. ed.). Shawnee Mission, KS: Autism Asperger Publishing Company.

Myles, B., Trautman, M., & Schelvan, R. (2004). *The hidden curriculum – Practical solutions for understanding unstated rules in social situations*. Shawnee Mission, KS: Autism Asperger Publishing Company.

Nowicki, S. Jr., & Duke, M. (1999). *Helping the child who doesn't fit in*. Atlanta, GA: Peachtree Publishers.

Obeidallah, D., & Earls, F. (1999). *Adolescent girls: The role of depression in delinquency*. National Institute of Justice Research Preview. Retrieved October 16, 2006, from http://www.ncjrs.gov/pdffiles1/fs000244.pdf

Paradiz, V. (2002). *Elijah's cup: A family's journey into the community and culture of high-functioning autism and Asperger's Syndrome*. New York: Free Press.

Seligman, M., & Darling, R. (1999). *Ordinary families, special children*. New York: Guilford Press.

Seligman, M. (1996). *The optimistic child*. New York: HarperCollins.

Siegel, L. M. (1999). *The complete IEP guide*. Berkeley, CA: Nolo Press.

Simpson, W. (2007). *My Andrew: Day-to-day living with a child with an autism spectrum disorder.* Shawnee Mission, KS: Autism Asperger Publishing Company.

Stewart, K. (2002). *Helping a child with nonverbal learning disorder* or *Asperger's Syndrome*. Oakland, CA: New Harbinger Publications, Inc.

Szatmari, P., Bremmer, R., & Nagy, J. N. (1989a). Asperger's Syndrome: A review of clinical features. *Canadian Journal of Psychiatry, 34*(6), 554-560.

Tantam, D. (1988). Annotation: Asperger's syndrome. *Journal of Child Psychology and Psychiatry, 29*, 836-840.

Trott, M. C. (2002). *Oh behave! Sensory processing and behavioral strategies*. Oxford, UK: The Psychological Corporation.

U.S. Department of Education. (n.d.). *My child's special needs: A guide to the individualized education program*. Retrieved December 30, 2006, from http://www.ed.gov/parents/needs/speced/iepguide/index.html

Vignola, D. *Semantic pragmatic disorder*. Retrieved October 13, 2006, from www.geocities.com/denisev2

Whitney, R. V. (2002). *Bridging the gap: Raising a child with nonverbal learning disorder*. New York: Perigee Books.

Wing, L. (1981). Asperger's syndrome: A clinical account. *Psychological Medicine, 11*, 115-130.

Index

Index

Index

Index

APC

P.O. Box 23173
Shawnee Mission, Kansas 66283-0173
www.asperger.net